Pascal for Micros

Mike James

Newnes Technical Books

Newnes Technical Books
is an imprint of the Butterworth Group
which has principal offices in
London, Boston, Durban, Singapore, Sydney, Toronto, Wellington

First published 1983

© **Butterworth & Co. (Publishers) Ltd, 1983**
Borough Green, Sevenoaks, Kent TN15 8PH, England

British Library Cataloguing in Publication Data

James, Mike
   Pascal for Micros.
   1. Pascal (Computer program language)
   2. Microcomputers—Programming
   I. Title
   001.64'24   QA76.73.P2

   ISBN 0-408-01249-8

Typeset by Phoenix Photosetting, Chatham
Printed in England by J. W. Arrowsmith Ltd., Bristol

Preface

Pascal is one of many computer languages that have become better known since the introduction of personal microcomputers. Perhaps the best known is BASIC, mainly bcause it is supplied as standard with most machines. It is difficult to decide how popular BASIC would be if every micro was delivered without software and every user had to choose (and pay for!) a computer language. It is certainly true that the second most popular language is Pascal and this observation carries even more force when it is realised that Pascal is an extra on most machines.

Why then do so many people make an active choice in favour of Pascal? There are many reasons but the most important is that Pascal is a rich language that is capable of handling both simple and advanced problems with economy. It is therefore a good first language to learn, because it will take you a long way before you have to look round for another language! Pascal is good for nearly all applications—scientific, technical and commercial—and if you're programming for fun then Pascal will increase your enjoyment.

However there is a small price to be paid for these advantages. If you are a complete beginner then you might find Pascal a little more difficult in the first stages. The reason for this is that learning a computer language is easier once you have written your first program. In Pascal the knowledge that you have to acquire to write even the simplest program is more than for a language such as BASIC. In other words there is an initial knowledge barrier that the complete beginner has to overcome before learning becomes easier and faster. To overcome this problem Chapters 1 and 2 spend some time introducing general ideas and give an overview of what a Pascal program is like. So by the end of Chapter 2 you may not be able to write a program but you should be able to read one! Building on this advantage Chapters 3 and 4 introduce the fundamental building blocks of Pascal—data types and control statements. Chapter 5 brings all the previous ideas together by way of three examples that are explained in detail. The purpose of this chapter is not only to explain how Pascal is used but also how programs in general are written. The remainder of the book deals with everything else you need to know about the slightly more advanced features of Pascal and includes a second chapter of fully explained example programs.

If you are completely new to computing then it is difficult for any book to tell you all you need to know about getting started. To overcome this problem I would suggest that you try to make friends with your computer by using it with the language it speaks most readily—this is most likely to be BASIC. Even if you have decided that Pascal is going to be your first computer language do not shy away from using whatever is available to familiarise yourself with your computer. It is a lot easier to learn Pascal if you have mastered the keyboard and know how to correct any typing errors that you might make.

If you are familiar with BASIC then you won't suffer the same problems as a complete beginner. You will know what a computer is and what it does. However you might find many of the ideas in Pascal difficult to learn because you are looking for BASIC-like facilities. In particular, you may find the lack of a **GOTO** (until Chapter 11) difficult to fathom. Writing Pascal programs does require a different frame of mind from writing BASIC so do not try to transfer BASIC methods to Pascal!

Learning any language is a matter of some study and much practice. This is no less true of learning a computer language. This book is designed to teach you the computer language Pascal but it will only achieve its objective if you are prepared both to read it and to write programs. To aid in this process a number of questions have been included at the end of each chapter, answers to which can be found at the back of the book. The questions have been designed to be easy to answer if you have understood the ideas contained in the chapter. If you feel in need of more testing problems then the best idea is to try to extend the example programs. Although the answers are given, you should feel free to improve on the programs suggested—there is rarely only one right answer in programming!

M. J.

Contents

1
All about Pascal

The desire to be able to program a computer has become increasingly widespread since the introduction of low-cost microcomputers. As most of these machines come equipped with a version of the language BASIC, the ability to program has so far tended to confine itself to this one language. There are many who would say that this is a very sad state of affairs because BASIC is a terrible language to program in! They then usually go on to explain that it is only possible to write GOOD programs in a language such as Pascal. I would not go so far in either damning BASIC or exalting Pascal. It is possible to write good programs in any language! What is important about Pascal is that it is a more sophisticated language than BASIC. If you are programming either for fun or for profit then familiarity with Pascal will provide you with exciting and challenging ways of thinking about your problems.

The history of Pascal

The computer language Pascal was invented in 1970 by Professor Niklaus Wirth of Zurich. It was named after the French mathematician, Blaise Pascal, who invented one of the earliest known calculators—a forerunner of the modern computer. As with all computer languages Pascal was designed to meet a particular objective. In this case the objective was to create a language which would be better suited to teaching programming than any existing language. As a teaching language it proved successful and it soon became popular for other applications. Perhaps the most important factor in the rise of Pascal's popularity was its adoption by the University of California, San Diego (UCSD) in 1973–74. After choosing Pascal as their main teaching language UCSD went on to produce an implementation of Pascal for a wide range of machines, both minis and micros. This availability of one version of Pascal on many different machines is an obvious advantage to anyone wanting to learn just one version of a language or write programs for as large an audience as possible.

Although Pascal was invented in 1970 this is not to say that it came out of the blue and had no similarity to computer languages that already existed—Pascal's ancestors include the programming languages ALGOL and PL1. Pascal took much of the best material from these two languages and as a result it is a better and simpler language than either.

Learning Pascal

As with all good things there is a price to be paid for the increased richness and sophistication of Pascal. Although Pascal is a suitable language for a beginner it does contain a number of advanced and powerful ideas. Fortunately it is possible to avoid these ideas until a good grasp of elementary Pascal is achieved. A more awkward problem is that you need to know rather more about Pascal before you can write your first program than with BASIC. This can mean that Pascal is a slower language to learn. In an attempt to overcome this difficulty, Chapter 2 gives an overview of a Pascal program and then Chapters 3 and 4 go over the same material in more detail. It is important to realise, especially if Pascal is going to be your first introduction to a computer language, that there is an initial 'knowledge barrier'. As you read Chapter 2 do not expect to be able to write a program by the time you reach the end. Rather than producing a sudden change from being a non-programmer to a programmer, learning Pascal results in a gradual improvement in programming skill. You move gradually into the state of being able to program and then, as you learn more, gradually into being an expert programmer!

If at any point in mastering Pascal you find that at first reading there is too much material to understand, don't give up and don't spend hours in deep study! Instead leave the subject for a few hours (or even a day) and do something different. When you return you should find that it all 'falls into place'. The reason for the effectiveness of this 'burst' type of learning is that understanding a programming language can often involve mastering a number of simple ideas at the same time. To see the whole picture you have to understand all of these simple ideas and if you misunderstand just one then the whole can seem much more complicated than it really is. Pausing gives time for the ideas that you have understood to consolidate and when you return to the subject the remaining ideas often slot into place with very little extra effort.

Which Pascal?

Unlike BASIC, Pascal is not usually supplied as a standard feature in most microcomputers. This means that before you can begin to learn or use Pascal you must choose and buy a version of the language to suit your machine. For some computers the choice is limited to one or two versions but for others the choice is very wide. If you are in the lucky position of using a machine that already has Pascal then the question of which version to use has been answered for you, but it is important that you know which particular version of Pascal you have and that you are aware that there are others which may be different. A description of five different and popular versions of Pascal is given at the end of this chapter.

No matter which version of Pascal you are using, you have to know how to input and run a program. Unfortunately each version has its own way of doing things. The programming language Pascal is fairly standard but there is no fixed way of getting a program into a computer and then running it. It is important not to confuse any difficulty of entering and running a program with difficulties in understanding and using a language. The first kind of difficulty is like not being able to find a sharp pencil and the second is like not being able to spell!

Before becoming too involved with learning Pascal it is a good idea to make sure that you can enter and run a program. This is done in such different ways for each version of Pascal that the only help that can be given here is to explain (in the next section) the general ways in which computers handle programs. This discussion will also help you understand the advantages and disadvantages of the various versions of Pascal. However, for detailed instructions on running programs consult the manual that comes with your Pascal in conjunction with the manual that comes with your computer.

Running programs

So far we have used the term computer language without really explaining what is meant. Computers have to be given a list of instructions before they can do what we want them to. The list of instructions is more usually called a program. Unfortunately the only language that a computer understands directly is very difficult for humans to cope with. Also every computer has its own native language or machine code which would mean learning a new language every time you changed to a different computer. To overcome these problems we use a so-called high level language, which is a

mixture of English and mathematics, to write programs which are
then converted to machine code by another program called a compiler.

Pascal is a high level language and before a program written in
Pascal can be run on a computer it must be translated to machine
code. This means that running a Pascal program takes at least three
operations:

1. The program must be entered into the computer as text.
2. It must be compiled into machine code.
3. It must then be run, i.e. the computer must begin obeying its
instructions.

The first stage usually involves the use of a program called an editor,
which allows text of any sort to be entered, altered and saved for
later use. The second stage then uses the output from the editor and
converts it to machine code. Finally this machine code is loaded into
the computer and is allowed to take control. We can visualise this
process as:

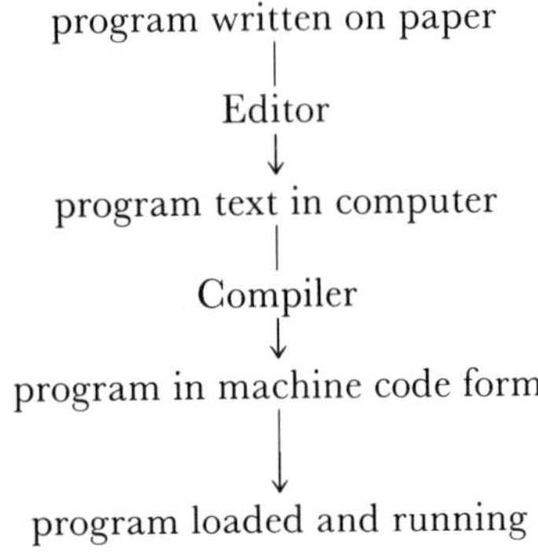

We start with a program written on paper and end with the equivalent machine code program in control of the computer's actions.

In developing a program it is rare for it to work first time. In this
case we have to discover the reason for the failure and correct it.
This involves going back to the text of the program and using the
editor to make the correction. The amended program must then be
re-compiled and once again tested by running. This forms a cycle
that may have to be repeated several times.

If you have used a microcomputer with a language such as
BASIC you may be puzzled as to why Pascal requires so many steps
to get from a written program to a running program. It is fairly common to find implementations of BASIC where the program is typed
in, edited and run without any obvious moving from editor to com-

piler, etc. The reason for this is that BASIC is most often implemented by an interpreter. An interpreter is a program that serves the same purpose as a compiler, in that it allows instructions written in a high level language to control a computer that understands only machine code, but it achieves this in a very different way. An interpreter is a program that is in the machine at the *same time* as the text of your program. When you type RUN, or whatever word indicates that the computer should carry out your program, the interpreter looks at the first line of your program and makes the machine carry out actions that are implied by its meaning. You can think of this as the interpreter converting the current line of your program to machine code and running it whereas a compiler converts the entire program before you can run it.

It is obvious that for learning a language it is better to use an interpreter or some similar system. It is a sad fact that nearly all implementations of Pascal use compilers (TCL Pascal is one notable exception; see below) and are therefore not ideal for beginners. However, if you need a program to be obeyed at full speed then use of a compiler is clearly the better choice. This is because an interpreter translates the program every time it is run but a compiler does it once only. Thus, for a program that uses an interpreter, the translation time is added to the time that the program takes to carry out its task. Therefore, while interpreters are easy to use, compilers produce fast programs.

The picture that we have given so far is a little too simple to account for the way that all versions of Pascal are implemented. The truth is that a compiler is a program that translates from one computer language to another—not just to machine code. It would for example be quite possible to write a compiler to change Pascal into BASIC. Indeed this might be an advantage because if we translated Pascal into BASIC we could make use of the BASIC interpreter that is almost always supplied with a microcomputer.

What we have just proposed is a method that is used by many versions of Pascal although instead of translating to BASIC the language that the compiler translates to is known as P-Code. In other words, many Pascal compilers do not translate Pascal into machine code: instead they produce another language called P-Code. This P-Code program is then interpreted by a P-Code interpreter. This might sound like a silly way to run a program because it combines the difficulty of a compiler in the first stage with the slowness of an interpreter in the second. However, it is the method used by a number of Pascal implementations (UCSD for example) and the reason is that it makes it easier to produce versions for different machines. If a compiler produces machine code then moving it to a new machine means virtually rewriting it. If a compiler produces P-Code then moving it to a new machine is a matter of writing a new P-Code interpreter—which is a considerably easier task!

To summarise, there are two popular ways to implement Pascal: compile to machine code, or compile to P-Code and then interpret it. Of course any one version of Pascal will only use one of these two methods but it should help you to understand the different steps that you have to go through to run your Pascal programs and why other versions are different.

A standard for Pascal

With all this discussion of differences between versions of Pascal you may be wondering which version of Pascal you should learn? There are two standards for Pascal. The first is simply the first-ever version of Pascal introduced by Wirth and the second is a definition of Pascal agreed by an international standards organisation (ISO) committee. Only one of the microcomputer versions of Pascal (Pascal/MT+) implements the ISO standard and none follows the original Wirth definition. However, they do agree on most aspects of implementation.

Rather than deal with either of the standard versions this book introduces a version of Pascal that is as close as possible to that used by most micros. If you use the Pascal described in this book you should find that your programs should work with most practical versions of Pascal. Sometimes you will find that a version will offer extra features that could make programs easier and shorter. You can find out about such extra features from the manual supplied with your Pascal, but be warned—if you make use of extras then your programs may not work on other machines. This may not worry you, in which case by all means discover the full range of the Pascal that you are using but, in any case, it will be considerably easier after you have mastered the Pascal described in the rest of the book! There are some places where the differences between the various versions of Pascal cannot be avoided. In the very few places where this happens the differences will be described and appropriate modifications will have to be made to any example programs given to make sure that they will work on your version of Pascal.

Summary

In this section of the chapter the idea of Pascal as a programming language has been introduced. The ways of implementing a computer language in general, and Pascal in particular, were also discussed. Finally, the problems produced by the existence of a number of versions of Pascal were examined.

Questions

Before moving on to the next section:

1. Discover which version of Pascal you are using.

2. If your version of Pascal has a compiler find out how to use the editor supplied with your system.

3. Find out how to run a program with your particular version of Pascal from the manual supplied with it.

Five Pascals for micros

A brief outline of five implementations of Pascal is given below. Inclusion in this list does not mean that the implementation is particularly recommended nor does exclusion imply disapproval. The five described below are simply either popular versions of Pascal or are for popular microcomputers.

UCSD Pascal

We have already mentioned how important this version of Pascal is in the section on History. This version is available for nearly every microcomputer and a number of minis. In particular, it is usually regarded as the standard Pascal for the Apple and in this context is better known simply as Apple Pascal. Apart from the Apple UCSD Pascal can also be used with any Z80/8080, 6502, 9900, 8086, 68000 or 6800/6809 systems (with a minimum of 48K of memory and a floppy disk system with at least 175 Kbytes of storage). The importance of UCSD Pascal is that it is possible to write a program on one machine and move it to another without any changes. Indeed, the motto of Softech Systems who distribute UCSD is 'One Pascal for ALL microcomputers'.

The most noticeable difference between UCSD Pascal and any other is that UCSD uses its own operating system. An operating system is simply a program that looks after the routine operation of a computer—creating and deleting files on disk, handling the keyboard and screen, etc. The best-known example of an operating system is probably CP/M but users of Apple will know DOS and TRS-80 users will know TRSDOS. The trouble with UCSD providing a new operating system is that it replaces the one that you may have spent time getting used to!

UCSD Pascal is compiled to an intermediate P-code form and then interpreted. As the final code is interpreted this makes UCSD slower than some other versions of Pascal but only by a factor of about two.

Pascal M

From the user's point of view this version of Pascal is nearly identical to UCSD Pascal except for the fact that it uses the standard operating systems—CP/M 2.0, MP/M or Cromemco's CDOS. It is only available for 8080/Z80-based machines and requires at least 56K of memory and one disk drive. If you use one of the above-named operating systems then Pascal M provides an attractive alternative choice to UCSD.

Pascal M is compiled to an intermediate P-Code and then interpreted. As in the case of UCSD this causes programs to run more slowly under Pascal M than under other Pascals.

Pascal MT+

It is important not to confuse Pascal/M with Pascal/MT+. They are very different products! Pascal/MT+ is a true compiler producing Z80 or 8080 machine code. This produces fast programs that are ideal for real time or production software. The other important fact about Pascal/MT+ is that it is currently the only Pascal for micros that claims to meet the ISO standard. Pascal/MT+ requires an 8080 or a Z80-based machine using CP/M 2.2 with a minimum of 52 Kbytes of memory and 140K of floppy disk storage.

Pascal/Z

Pascal/Z is like Pascal/MT+ in that it produces machine code but it has some important differences. The most important is that it only produces Z80 code and thus it is not available on as many machines as Pascal/MT+. Another difference is that the machine code is produced in two stages. First the compiler outputs macro assembler and then this is converted to machine code by using the assembler supplied. This two-stage process may be a disadvantage when first learning Pascal—it takes longer to try a program out—but it can be an advantage if you want to mix assembler and Pascal. Pascal/Z runs under CP/M 2.2 and requires a Z80-based machine with at least 54 Kbytes of RAM and one disk drive.

TCL Pascal

TCL Pascal is a Pascal compiler that is very popular on the Commodore PET range of computers. It is different from all the previous versions of Pascal in that it can be used in one of two modes—memory-resident or as a disk-based compiler. The memory-resident mode is ideal for learning Pascal because a program can be typed in and run in one step. The disk-based mode is necessary if you want to write large programs because in the memory-resident mode RAM is taken up by the compiler.

TCL Pascal contains many extensions to allow the special features of the PET to be used without resorting to machine code. The minimum requirements for TCL Pascal are a 32K PET and a Commodore dual disk drive (note that the disk is required to run the memory-resident mode as well as the disk-based mode).

The five Pascals at a glance

Name	Micro type	Op. sys	Speed	Machine type	Approx cost
UCSD	6502/Z90/ 8080/8096/ 6800/6809/ 9900	own	slow	most	£250
M	Z80/8080	CP/M	slow	any CP/M	£150
MT+	Z80/8080	CP/M	fast	any CP/M	£250
Z	Z80	CP/M	fast	any Z80/CPM	£200
TCL	6502	PET	slow	PET	£120

2

The Pascal program

In this chapter the idea of a Pascal program is introduced. As you read through don't worry too much about detail; try instead to see the general nature of things. There is plenty of time for detail in the rest of the book! One of the problems of learning Pascal is that you have to know a certain amount before you can even begin to write the simplest of programs. By the end of this chapter you should be able at least to appreciate the workings of a small program and identify its different parts. It is important that you try to run this short program on your computer to discover if you have acquired the knowledge outlined in Chapter 1 about editing and running programs.

Anatomy of a program

In general, a computer program consists of two parts: a definition section and an instruction section. The instruction section is the part that most people think of as *the* program. It is a list of instructions that the computer will carry out when the program is run. The definition section is where the programmer defines the objects—data etc—that the instruction section will operate on. In many computer languages the definition section is mixed up with the instruction section, which may give the impression that the program consists of one long list of instructions. Pascal, however, separates the two sections very clearly and this is an important feature of a Pascal program. To illustrate this point, and to make an early start on understanding Pascal, let's consider a short program:

```
PROGRAM sum;
VAR total,number1,number2:INTEGER;
BEGIN
        number1 := 4;
        number2 :=3;
        total := number1 + number2
END.
```

If you examine this program you should be able to understand what it is trying to do without any extra explanation—it is adding 4 to 3!

There are some other simple things that we can learn from this program. The words written in capitals are part of the Pascal language and do not have to be defined. The words written in lower case are not part of the Pascal language and their meaning has to be defined within the program. If you look at the part of the program between the **BEGIN** and **END.** you should be able to see that this is the instruction part of the program. It tells the computer to do things to 'number1', 'number2' and 'total'. To understand what it tells the computer to do you first have to know more about the nature of 'number1', 'number2' and 'total'.

The first statement of the program simply gives the program a name—in this case 'sum'. The second statement is the definition section of the program. It lets the computer, and the reader, know that the three objects, 'number1', 'number2' and 'total'. are INTEGERS. (An integer is a whole number, e.g. 0, 1, -3, 5, but not 1.2, -3.3.) The first word of the statement, **VAR**, gives us the additional information that they are variables—that is, they can change their values in the instruction section of the program. (The idea of a variable is also covered in the next section.) The first statement following the **BEGIN** sets 'number1' to the value 4, the second sets 'number2' to the value 3 and the third sets 'total' to number1 + number2, i.e. 7. At this stage don't worry if you don't understand it in detail; the only thing that is important is that you see that there are two parts to the program—definition and instruction.

All Pascal programs take this general form:

PROGRAM name
    definitions
BEGIN
    instructions
END.

Variables and type

One of the most important ideas in programming is the variable. A variable is the simplest way of using the computer's memory to store information for later use. It is useful to think of a computer memory as being made up of a number of boxes. Each box can be given a name—often called its identifier—and can be used to store some item of data. Such a named box is called a variable. In the previous example 'number1', 'number2' and 'total' are all examples of variables. It is good if you can get into the habit now of thinking of a variable as an identifier, e.g. 'number1', and a box that the computer associates with it. To emphasise this, Pascal uses a special symbol := to mean 'store in the memory box'. For example:

    number1 := 4

could be read as 'store the number 4 in the memory box CALLED number1'. More properly, the symbol := is known as assignment and the above example would be read by someone used to programming and to Pascal in particular as 'assign the value 4 to the variable number1'. However you read the statement you should never forget the idea of storing something in a box.

Now that you know better what a variable is you should be able to understand better the purpose of the definition part of Pascal program. When you write

VAR number1:INTEGER

you are asking the computer to reserve for you a box suitable for storing integers and to label that box 'number1'. The things that you can store in a box are restricted to the type that you specify when you define the variable. For example, you cannot try to store a number with a fractional part in an INTEGER variable; this would be like trying to store oranges in egg boxes. In the context of the above program a statement like:

    number1 := 3.256

would make the computer generate an error message to tell you that this was impossible and then stop.

This may seem a little unreasonable. Why can't the computer provide a box of the correct type to store whatever we want? This is of course possible and some other computer languages do allow you to ignore the problem of matching the type of box to the type of thing that you want to store in it, but Pascal is not one of these. Apart from one notable exception (see Chapter 3), Pascal demands that the variable type and what you try to store in it must be compatible. The reason for this is that it makes it easier to spot logical errors that might have found their way into your program. If you expect some data to be of a particular type and it turns out not to be, then you have made a mistake. In other words Pascal forces you to think carefully about the types of data that your program will work with.

All of this discussion leaves the question of what types of data a Pascal program can handle completely unanswered. The only data type that we have introduced so far is INTEGER and this is all that we shall use until the next chapter where the other basic data types

will be introduced. It is sufficient for the moment to say that Pascal
has enough data types for nearly all programming situations!

There is one last thing left to say about variable and data types.
What you can do with a variable in the instruction part of a program
depends on what sort of variable it is. In the earlier example we used
the + sign to indicate that 'number1' should be added to 'number2'
and the result assigned to 'total', but it should be noticed that this
only makes sense if all the variables are of a type that the operation
of addition can be applied to. What this means is that as we introduce new data types in Chapter 3 it will be necessary for us to look at
the types of operations that we can carry out on them. This may
sound very complicated but because most of the operations are
obvious, for example you can add INTEGERs, it turns out to be not
so bad. However, there are a few surprises in store.

Compound statements

The instruction part of a Pascal program is made up of a list of
simple statements between the words **BEGIN** and **END.** Although
in the previous example each statement started on a new line this is
not necessary. Pascal uses the semicolon to separate statements and
the way that you place statements on lines is up to you. For example,
the instruction part of the sum program can just as well be written:

BEGIN
number1:=4;number2:=3;total:=number1+number2
END.

The order in which the statements will be carried out by the computer is the same as the natural order of reading them, that is left to
right and top to bottom. Notice that, although the semicolon is used
as a statement separator, not every Pascal statement ends with a
semicolon. For example, the statement before the **END** doesn't have
a semicolon after it because **END** isn't a Pascal statement.

You may be wondering what the purpose of the **BEGIN** and
END is. It is an important feature of Pascal that any collection of
statements can be grouped together using **BEGIN** and **END** and
such a group will be treated as a single statement, known as a compound statement. This is important because it allows us to take a
number of small actions already available in Pascal and, by putting
a **BEGIN** and an **END** around them, we can think of the result as a
brand-new single action. If you are trying to solve a large problem
then it is obviously a good idea to try to solve it in small parts. If you
look at a Pascal program you will now be able to see that the instruction part is a single (compound) statement. The full stop at the end

of the program indicates that the program is finished. If the program is a large one and you look at it more closely, you will most certainly discover that some of the statements between the **BEGIN** and **END** are also compound statements. In this sense, writing a Pascal program is a process of building larger and larger compound statements until you have a single statement that will solve your problem—that is, the program!

A complete example—input and output

The short example of a Pascal program given earlier is not at all useful in that it adds two numbers together but keeps the result to itself. Before we move on to consider the details of Pascal it would be useful to look at another example of a program, but this time one that can be run and checked on your computer. To do this we need to add two things to our knowledge of Pascal—how to get data into and out of our program. The easier of the two to understand is getting data out of a program. Pascal uses the statement,

    WRITE(variable name)

to display the contents of a variable on the computer's screen. For example,

    WRITE(total)

is an instruction to the computer to print the number stored in the variable 'total'. For the moment don't worry about where or how the number will be printed on the screen. This will be covered in more detail in Chapter 8.

The problem of getting data into the program is just as easily solved by using the

    READ(variable name)

statement, but in practice this can cause a lot of trouble for beginners. There are, in general, two ways of causing data to be stored in a variable. The first method we met briefly earlier in this chapter—the assignment statement. The second we have just introduced in the form of the READ statement. To save a lot of confusion later on it is important to understand the difference between these two methods of placing data in variables.

If you write

    number1 := 3

in a program, when the computer reaches this instruction all it does is to store the number 3 in the variable called 'number1'. It then carries on and executes the next instruction. If you write

READ(number1)

then, when the computer reaches this instruction, it pauses and gives the user the opportunity to input a number at the computer's keyboard. The number typed in is then stored in the variable and the computer moves on to the next instruction.

The essential difference between the two methods is that assignment is a way of moving data around inside the program while input brings new data in from outside the program. The details of how the computer actually takes input from the outside world varies from machine to machine; some will just wait for you to type a number, others will print a question mark to show that the computer is waiting. Older machines do not even take input from a keyboard: they expect you to put your data on punched cards.

If you type a number in response to a READ statement, there must be some way to indicate that you have finished typing. For example, if you type 124 in response to a READ, the computer does not know whether you're taking a long time to think of the next digit or whether you have finished and 124 is all you're going to type! The solution to this problem is that pressing the space key or the key marked Return or Enter is taken to mean 'I have finished typing the number'. So, type in your number and, when you have finished, press Space or Return. The important thing is that all computers have some way of reading data into a running program. Using the example program given below you should be able to find out how yours behaves.

There is one other small thing that we have to know before we can write our example and this concerns the naming of the program. In our first example the statement,

PROGRAM sum

was used to give the program the name sum. However, the **PROGRAM** statement has other uses than just naming a program. It is used to tell the computer that you are going to want to carry out some input and/or output of data. To be more accurate, it tells the computer where to send the data from a WRITE statement and where to get the data for a READ statement. All that you need to know for now is that if you are going to use READ and WRITE statements in your program then the PROGRAM statement should take the form:

PROGRAM name(INPUT,OUTPUT)

This will make your program READ from the normal keyboard and WRITE to the screen.

At last we can introduce a complete example. The following program adds 3 to any number:

```
PROGRAM addthree(INPUT,OUTPUT);
VAR number1,number2,total:INTEGER;
BEGIN
        number1 := 3;
        READ(number2);
        total := number1 + number2;
        WRITE(total)
END.
```

You should be able to understand most of this program. The first statement gives the program the name 'addthree' and establishes the normal input and output. The second statement forms the definition part of the program and tells us that 'number1', 'number2' and 'total' are going to be integers. The instruction part of the program can be found between the **BEGIN** and **END**. Following this through line by line, first 3 is stored in the variable called 'number1', then the computer pauses while someone types a number on the keyboard. This is then stored in the variable called 'number2'. The third line adds the *contents* of the two variables 'number1' and 'number2' and places the result in the variable called 'total'. The final instruction prints the contents of the variable 'total' on the screen so that we can see the answer.

This is a very simple program but if you can understand what it is doing and identify the purpose of its two parts then you are well on your way to understanding Pascal. It is important that you try to run this program on your computer before you move on to the other chapters in this book. There are two reasons for this. First, it is essential that you discover *how* to enter and run a Pascal program and second it is important that you see the program reading data in to make sure that you understand what happens. Try entering letters and fractions to find out what your version of Pascal does when you make a mistake. In short, use this example to become familiar with your computer and Pascal.

Summary

In this chapter the two parts of a Pascal program, the definition section and the instruction section, have been introduced. The idea of a variable was discussed along with the two ways of putting data into a variable—the assignment statement and the READ statement. The use of **BEGIN** and **END** to form a compound statement was described and finally a short example Pascal program was given.

Questions

1. Draw the line that separates the definition and instruction parts of the 'addthree' program.

2. How many compound statements are there in the instruction part of 'addthree'?

3. Change the 'addthree' program into an 'addfive' program and run your answer to test it.

4. Change the 'addthree' program into a general addition program by READing 'number1' as well as 'number2' and run your answer to test it.

3
Variables and assignment, data types and expressions

In the first part of this chapter we look in detail at variables, the names that we can use to identify them and the fundamental data types that Pascal provides. In the second part we look at expressions, that is the ways in which data can be manipulated.

Variables and identifiers

As was discussed in Chapter 2, a variable is a named area of storage. There are two ways in which variables can differ—in name and in type. The name that you give to a variable is known as an identifier and there are certain rules that govern what constitutes a valid identifier.

1. An identifier must begin with a letter; this may be followed by a mixture of letters and numbers but it must not contain any other character, e.g. a full stop or a comma.
2. Some implementations of Pascal impose an upper limit on the length of an identifier.
3. Most implementations of Pascal will allow identifiers of at least eight characters.
4. An identifier must not be a Pascal reserved word (see Appendix 1 for a list of reserved words).

In practice these rules are not too restrictive. If we use identifiers of eight characters or less then we can be sure that our programs will run on most versions of Pascal. The only rule that might need some explanation is the last one. A Pascal reserved word is part of Pascal's standard vocabulary, for example **BEGIN** or **END**. If you were allowed identifiers that were the same as these words it would be difficult to work out the meaning of lines like:

BEGIN BEGIN:=1 **END**

A full list of reserved words can be found in Appendix 1. Meanwhile, note that they appear in **CAPITALS IN BOLD TYPE**.

Identifiers crop up as names for things other than variables so it is worth studying the rules in some detail. The following are all valid identifiers: total, day, item2, t1d3. The following are invalid: 1day, item.2, end. The reasons why these are invalid are: the first starts with a number; the second contains a character other than a letter or a digit (a full stop); and the third is a reserved word. From now on whenever reference is made to an identifier it should be taken to mean a name made up according to the above rules.

Obviously the name that you give to a variable (or anything else for that matter) should reflect its use. For example, if a variable is going to be used to store the results of calculating the area of a circle then it makes sense to call it 'area'. The trouble starts when you come to write a real program; finding appropriate, meaningful names is a knack that some people seem to have and others don't. It is, however, worth patience and effort; choosing a suitable name for everything can make a program much easier to read and understand.

Variables and assignment

The whole reason for having variables is the storage of data. Pascal uses the double symbol := as a way of storing data in a variable. A statement such as

    count := 3

should be read as 'store 3 in the variable called count' or 'set the current value of count to 3'. A more sophisticated way of saying the same thing is 'assign the 3 to the variable count' and this gives us the usual name for this type of statement—it is called an assignment statement and := is known as the assignment operator. In general there is always a variable to the left of the assignment operator but there can be a wide variety of things to the right. For example:

    count := 3;
    total := count;
    count := total + 1

If you examine these three statements you will see that there is always a variable name to the left but the right-hand side is different in each case. The first statement simply stores 3 in 'count', the second transfers the contents of the variable 'count' into the variable 'total' and the third adds one to the contents of 'total' and stores the result in 'count'. The thing that is the same about each of the right-hand sides is that each of them in some way produces a data value that is stored in the variable on the left. The right-hand side is often referred to as an expression; the production of a data value from it is known as evaluating the expression. In the first statement the expression is very simple indeed—it is just 3—and evaluation is trivial. The second and third statements are a little more complicated in that the need to evaluate them is more obvious. Evaluation of the second is simply retrieving the contents of a variable, and evaluation of the third involves adding one to the contents of a variable.

The idea of assigning the result of evaluating an expression is fundamental to computer programming. What form an expression can take depends on what type of data is involved—for example, you can add numbers but not letters—and we will return to what makes a valid expression each time we introduce a new data type.

Data types—the VAR statement

Apart from giving a variable a name it is also necessary to decide on its type. The type of a variable governs what sort of data you can store in it. Pascal is very fussy about data types and will give you an error message if you define a variable as being of one type and then try to store data of another type in it. You can define the type of a variable using the **VAR** statement:

VAR variable list : type

where 'variable list' is a list of variable identifiers separated by commas, and 'type' is the name of any valid Pascal data type. For example INTEGER is a valid data type (discussed in the next section) and

VAR count,cost,sum :INTEGER

is a correct **VAR** statement defining the three variables 'count', 'cost' and 'sum' as INTEGER. As well as defining a number of variables to be of a single type you can continue the statement and define other variable lists to be any valid type. For example, REAL is also a valid data type (discussed later) and

VAR count,cost,sum :INTEGER;
      area,rate:REAL;

is a valid **VAR** statement defining the two variables 'area' and 'rate' as REAL in addition to the three INTEGER variables defined by the previous statement. You can continue **VAR** statements in this way as often as necessary. If you are at all confused by this don't worry because there will be many examples in the rest of this chapter as the different data types are introduced.

Data type I—INTEGER

An integer is a whole number. The term whole number includes both positive and negative numbers and zero but not any number with a fractional part. For example 3, −3 and 0 are all integers, but 3.3, −4.1 and 0.4 are not integers. This may seem obvious but there is one complication: in Pascal a number like 3 is considered to be an integer but 3.0 is not.

Although 3 and 3.0 are equal they are not of the same type. One way of thinking about this is that 3.0 is a number whose fractional part just happens to be zero. Writing a decimal point is a sign that we are willing to consider the existence of a fractional part in the answer to questions. To illustrate this idea, consider these two seemingly simple questions. What is the next number larger than 3? Obviously, the answer is 4. However, were I to ask what is the next number larger than 3.0, this poses a much more difficult question. Is it 3.1 or 3.01 or 3.000000001, etc? In other words, although 3 and 3.0 are equal in value they are different types of number. In Pascal, writing a decimal point in a number guarantees that it is *not* an integer.

If you want to use a variable to store integers then it must be defined as INTEGER in a **VAR** statement. For example:

VAR count,max :INTEGER

defines both 'count' and 'max' to be INTEGER variables. If you try to store anything other than an integer in them you will be informed of your mistake!

Although in theory an integer can be as large as you please, in practice there will be a largest integer value that can be stored in a variable. This varies from computer to computer but Pascal gives it the standard name MAXINT. Any integer that you store in an INTEGER variable must be in the range:

−MAXINT . . . . . −2,−1,0,1,2 . . . . . MAXINT

MAXINT is normally quite large—for example, on many machines it is 32767—but you should be aware of the possibility of an error if an integer becomes too large. If MAXINT is 32767 then the following are valid integers −29000, 30000, 32767 and the following are invalid 34000, −32768, 64000. (Notice that MAXINT is not a variable and you cannot assign a new value to it. It is a named constant and will be discussed later.)

INTEGER expressions

It should come as no surprise that you can form arithmetic expressions with integers. However, there are some differences between a normal arithmetic expression and a Pascal integer expression. The operations that you can use on INTEGERs include:

+	addition
−	subtraction
*	multiply
DIV	integer divide
MOD	remainder

The first three operations should be familiar from standard arithmetic, the only difference being that the usual × sign for multiplication is replaced by the symbol *. The reason for this is that * is easier to read and allows the letter x to be used in variable names (identifiers). The last two are a little bit unusual and we will return to them in a moment. You can make up arithmetic expressions involving integers that look little different from standard arithmetic. For example;

    2*4+3
    count+1
    area−2*count+size

The first expression evaluates to 11. The result of the other two obviously depends on what is stored in the variables.

There is a problem in working out what an expression like 3+2*4 means. Is it three plus two (i.e. five), times four, making twenty, or is it two times four (i.e. eight), plus three, making eleven? This order of evaluation problem is common to all expressions, not just those to do with integers. For this reason a discussion of it is left to a later section. It is important to realise that this problem exists, however, when reading the examples in this and following sections. If there is any doubt about the meaning of an expression it can be made clear by the use of brackets:

    (3+2)*4
    3+(2*4)

The first expression evaluates to 20 and the second to 11. The rule is that you always work out brackets first.

You will have noticed that there is an operation missing from the list given above. We have addition, subtraction and multiplication but what about division? The trouble with dividing two integers is that the result might not be another integer. For example, 1 divided by 2 is .5, and .5 is not an integer. This is not the case with the other three operations. Adding, subtracting or multiplying two integers always gives another integer. Obviously, if you are evaluating an integer expression the result must be an integer so that it can be stored in an INTEGER variable. Division is too important to be left out of the range of things that you can do with integers. Pascal provides **DIV** and **MOD** to overcome these problems.

DIV is a division operation that always gives you an integer by ignoring any fractional part of the result. For example:

1 **DIV** 2
7 **DIV** 3

evaluate to 0 and 2 respectively. The reason for this is that 1 divided by 2 is 0.5, so ignoring the fractional part gives you zero, and 7 divided by 3 is 2.333, which gives 2 if you ignore the .333.

MOD is in a sense the other side of the coin in that it gives you the remainder. For example:

1 **MOD** 2
7 **MOD** 3

both evaluate to 1. The reason for this is that 2 'goes into' 1 zero times with the remainder 1, and 3 'goes into' 7 twice, remainder 1. Using **DIV** and **MOD** you can handle the division of integers in a very flexible way. **DIV** gives you the number of times something can be divided by something else and **MOD** gives you the remainder. Both obviously are integer answers.

Data type II—REAL

A real number is a number that may have a fractional part. For example, 3.23, 53.3434, −343.33 or 0.01 are all valid real numbers. Real numbers are closer to what we normally think of as numbers. Pascal recognises a number as real if it satisfies three conditions:

1. It must have a decimal point.
2. It must have at least one digit to the right of the decimal point.
3. It must have at least one digit to the left of the decimal point.

Because of these three rules there are numbers that we would normally regard as good examples of real numbers that Pascal would reject. For example 1. or .01 are not Pascal REALs because 1. doesn't have anything to the right of the decimal point and .01 doesn't have anything to the left. A REAL variable is one that can be used to store a real number and is defined by an appropriate **VAR** statement. For example:

VAR area,vat,percent:REAL

defines the variables 'area' 'vat' and 'percent' as REAL.

Although the best-known method of writing down real numbers is with a decimal point, this is sometimes inconvenient if there are a lot of zeros before or after the decimal point. For example .0000000001 is a little tedious to write down and likely to be entered incorrectly. To overcome this problem with very small and very large real numbers you can use exponential or scientific notation. The large number 1000000 could be described as 1 followed by 6 zeros. This can be written as 1.0E+6. In general you can write any real number in two parts—a number known as the mantissa and a number known as the exponent—with an E to separate them. To convert from this E notation back to the more usual notation all you have to do is follow these rules:

1. If the exponent N is positive move the decimal point in the mantissa N places to the RIGHT, writing zeros if necessary.
2. If the exponent is negative move the decimal point in the mantissa N places to the LEFT, writing zeros if necessary.

For example, 3.234E+6 becomes 3234000 and 33.323E−4 is .0033323. The only thing that you have to remember is that moving the decimal point one place to the right decreases the exponent by one, and one place to the left increases it by one. It is important to note that Pascal will always print out a real number in exponent form: do not ignore 'E' when it appears on a printout! (There is a way to print out REALs in the more usual form. This is discussed in Chapter 8 on Input/Output.)

Just as in the case of the INTEGERs the REALs have a restricted range. For the REALs, however, the situation is a little more complicated. There will not only be a maximum value that can be stored in the computer, but a minimum value as well. The reason for this is that REALs are stored inside the computer in a form similar to exponential notation. The mantissa and the exponent are stored only to a certain number of digits accuracy. If the mantissa is stored to 6 digits and the exponent is stored to two digits then the largest number that can be represented is 0.999999E99 and the smallest number is 0.000001E−99. (It is left as an exercise for the reader to convert these two numbers to the normal decimal notation!)

Real numbers can be combined to make expressions in much the same way as integers. The basic operations are:

> \+ addition
> − subtraction
> * multiplication
> / real division

The three operations +, −, and * are little different from the equivalent integer operations or from standard arithmetic. The only difference is in the use of / for division. Unlike the problems that we found with integer division, dividing a real number by a real number always gives another real number. Examples of real expressions are:

    3.3*4.0/2.1
    (3.1+1.0)/2.0+3.1
    (area + size/3.4)*6.1

Input and output of REAL and INTEGER

Although the subject of Input/Output (I/O) will be dealt with in detail in Chapter 8 it is difficult to avoid the use of READ and WRITE until then. A brief explanation of how READ and WRITE work was given in Chapter 2 but it is worth restating and enlarging on the ideas here.

The command

    READ(variable)

causes the computer to pause and wait for you to type a value that will then be assigned to the variable. The value that you input must be of the same type as the variable. In other words if 'variable' is of type INTEGER you must not include any decimal points or fractional parts in the number that you type at the keyboard.

It is important to remember that there are two ways of getting data into a variable. You can write an assignment statement or you can READ the value in. If you use an assignment statement then the same value will be assigned every time the program is run. If you use READ then you can type in a different value every time the program is run.

The statement

    WRITE(variable)

will print the value stored in 'variable' on the system's output device. The value will be displayed at the next available position. This may not always produce a very clear output but it is enough to see if a program is working. Later, in Chapter 8, we will see how the position and exact form of the output can be controlled, but to improve the readability of the output of some of the example programs it is worth knowing that the statement

WRITELN

will cause the next number to be printed on the next line. Treat WRITELN as meaning 'start a new line'.

Constants

Although we have spent a lot of time explaining the idea of a variable we have been using the equally important idea of a constant without any explanation. A constant is an explicit data value. For example, in

area:= 3.1

3.1 is a REAL constant, and in

sum:= 1034

1034 is an INTEGER constant. It should be clear that every data type has its own variety of constants. The idea of a constant may seem so obvious that there is no point in discussing it. However, you can give a name to a constant and this very useful feature of Pascal can cause confusion between variables and constants. A name can be given to a constant by using the **CONST** statement, the general form of which is:

```
CONST identifier = constant;
      identifier = constant;
           .    =    .
           .    =    .
           .    =    .
      identifier = constant
```

For example,

CONST pi = 3.14159;date = 82

defines the constants 'pi' and 'date'. Notice that = is used, not the assignment symbol :=. The type of a named constant is the same as the explicit constant and there is no need to declare the type of the constant that it represents. Thus, in the previous example 'pi' is a

REAL constant because 3.14159 is REAL and 'date' is an INTEGER constant because 82 is INTEGER.

It is important to realise that a named constant is different from a variable no matter how much they may appear to be the same. If 'date' is a constant, then

```
date:=date + 1
```

is wrong! A constant cannot change its value during the course of a program. Put another way, you cannot assign to a constant. However, you can use named constants in expressions. For example, the area of a circle is given by 3.141 times the radius squared. So, if 'area' and 'radius' are real variables, then

```
area:=3.141*radius*radius
```

can be used to calculate the area of a circle. But if we define a named constant 'pi' we can make this expression easier to read

```
area:=pi*radius*radius
```

It should come as no surprise to discover that the **CONST** statement belongs in the definition part of a program. To be precise, any **CONST** statement MUST come before any **VAR** statements. (The reason for this will become clear later.)

The complete program to calculate the area of a circle is:

```
PROGRAM circle (INPUT,OUTPUT);
CONST pi=3.141;
VAR area, radius:REAL;
BEGIN
        WRITELN;
        READ (radius);
        area:=pi*radius*radius;
        WRITELN;
        WRITE (area)
END.
```

You should by now be able to understand the different parts of this program, but it might be worth going through it line by line. The first line names the program 'circle' and tells the computer that we are going to do some input/output. The **CONST** statement defines 'pi' to be a REAL constant equal to 3.141. The **VAR** statement defines two REAL variables 'area' and 'radius'. The **BEGIN** signals that we have finished defining things and are ready to start doing something. The WRITELN starts a new line ready for the READ statement to wait while a REAL number is typed at the keyboard, and then stored in 'radius'. The next statement is an assignment statement. The expression to the right of the := is evaluated and the result is stored in 'area'. The next statement, WRITELN, starts a new line ready for the final statement of the program, WRITE (area), to print out the result.

Two points to note while running the program are: the number typed at the keyboard must be terminated by a space or by pressing the Return or Enter key; and the answer printed out will be in exponential form. Run the program a few times to make sure that you are completely familiar with the way it works.

Order of evaluation

All of the expressions that we have looked at so far share a common problem. No matter what type the variables are, an expression like

    sum+a*b

is ambiguous. Does it mean

    (sum+a)*b

i.e. do the addition before the multiplication, or

    sum+(a*b)

i.e. do the multiplication before the addition?

It's clear that the problem is the order of evaluation. If you know your simple algebra then it is possible that you're wondering what all the fuss is about—because in algebra multiplication is always done first. As it happens, Pascal's rules are similar to those of simple algebra.

The order in which an expression is to be evaluated is specified in Pascal by assigning priorities to the various operations and carrying out the highest priority operations first. For example, the priorities of the operations that we have introduced so far are:

Operator	Priority
* / **DIV MOD**	2
+ −	1 (lowest)

The only difficulty arrives when two operations of the same priority occur in the same expression. For example, in the expression 3*6/2 which should be carried out first—the * or the / ? Pascal solves the problem by evaluating such expressions from left to right. So 3*6/2 is evaluated as (3*6)/2. The complete list of rules for evaluating expressions is:

1. Work out any brackets first, starting at the left and working out any inner brackets as required.
2. Carry out highest priority operations first.
3. Work from left to right on operations of equal priority.

These rules are easier to use than they look but, if in doubt when writing expressions, use brackets to make your meaning clear.

A very common mistake made by beginners and experts alike is to translate expressions such as a/2b (meaning a divided by twice b) into a/2*b. Unfortunately the Pascal evaluation of this latter expression is equivalent to (a/2)*b, which is a divided by 2 and then multiplied by b, because equal priority operations are carried out from left to right. The correct way to write a/2b without using brackets is a/2/b, which is a divided by 2 and then divided by b. This example should convince you to use brackets if you are in any doubt about the meaning of an expression.

Expressions involving other operations are evaluated using the same rules and a full table of priorities can be found in Appendix 2.

Type conversion

There is obviously a connection between the INTEGER 3 and the REAL 3.0. Pascal provides a number of functions to allow conversion between REAL and INTEGER and vice versa.

A REAL value can be converted to an INTEGER in two different ways:

    x:=trunc(real)

which simply chops off the fractional part of a real number and assigns the resulting integer to 'x', and

    x:=round(real)

which converts a real number into an integer by rounding it up or down. So trunc(3.65) is the integer 3 and round(3.65) is the integer 4.

The conversion of an INTEGER to a REAL is carried out automatically. If you write

    x:=2

and 'x' is REAL then 2 will be converted into 2.0, a REAL. This automatic conversion is unique among the range of Pascal data types. It also extends to the use of INTEGER variables and constants in REAL expressions. For example:

x:=sum+2
x:=3.4+time*4

are valid if 'x' is REAL and 'sum' and 'time' are either INTEGER
or REAL. In short, this one relaxation of data types means that you
can mix INTEGERs and REALs in REAL expressions without
worry.

Summary

Some important and fundamental ideas have been introduced in this
chapter. The idea of variable and data type were discussed and two
particular data types, REAL and INTEGER, dealt with in detail.
The final themes of the chapter were expressions and their order of
evaluation.

Questions

1. Evaluate the following expressions:
   3*4+4*2
   2*(3−2)
   8 **DIV** 3
   8 **MOD** 3
   1/2

2. Write suitable definitions for variables to be used for storing:
   —the number of letters in a word;
   —the length of a piece of string;
   —the temperature of an oven;
   —the number of people on a bus.

3. Write a short program that will calculate and print the area of a
square given the length of one side. (See program 'circle' given
earlier.)

4
The flow of control

So far all the programs that we have written have been lists of instructions that the computer carries out one after the other. The order in which the instructions are carried out is from left to right and from top to bottom, in the same order that a human would read a program. The computer can only be carrying out one instruction at a time and it is sometimes useful to think of this instruction as controlling what the computer is doing. Thus, while a program is running, control passes from statement to statement and the way in which control passes through a program is known as the flow of control. This is easy to understand but the trouble is that this simple top-to-bottom/left-to-right flow of control isn't powerful enough to solve even simple problems. For example, suppose we want to read in and add together four numbers. The only way that we can do this using our present knowledge of Pascal is:

```
PROGRAM add(INPUT,OUTPUT);
VAR total,number:REAL;
BEGIN
        total:=0;
        READ(number);
        total:=total+number;
        READ(number);
        total:=total+number;
        READ(number);
        total:=total+number;
        READ(number);
        total:=total+number;
        WRITE(total)
END.
```

Reading in each number and adding it to the total using the pair of instructions,

```
READ(number);
total:=total+number
```

is just manageable for four numbers, but imagine the length of the program that adds 100 numbers together; and what if the number of numbers is variable? Both of these problems can be solved using the **FOR** statement.

The FOR statement

A single Pascal statement can be executed any number of times using a **FOR** statement. Before giving the general form of **FOR** it may be useful to look at a simple example:

```
PROGRAM loop (INPUT,OUTPUT);
VAR count:INTEGER;
    number:REAL;
BEGIN
    number :=5.5;
    FOR count:=1 TO 10 DO WRITE(number)
END.
```

This (not too useful) program prints the same variable ('number') ten times on the screen.

The meaning of the **FOR** statement can almost be understood by reading it. The WRITE statement is carried out ten times. The first time the variable 'count' is 1. The next time it is 2, and so on, until its value reaches 10 when the next instruction is carried out (i.e. the normal flow of control resumes). The variable 'count' is used to count the number of times that the statement has been repeated. You can make use of the variable 'count' just like any other variable. So, for example, you could change the loop program to read;

```
DO WRITE(count)
```

The general form of the **FOR** statement is:

```
FOR integer variable:=start value TO final value
                DO any statement
```

Notice that the variable used to count the number of times that the statement is carried out has to be of the type INTEGER. This variable is known as the index variable. The 'start' and 'final' values must also be of type INTEGER but they can be expressions or constants. If they are expressions they are evaluated only once at the start of the **FOR**. The value of the index variable can be used but must not be altered by the statement following the **DO**. Also the value of the index variable is undefined at the completion of the **FOR**. If the 'start value' is bigger than the 'final value', then the statement is not executed at all.

It may seem that the ability to repeat a single statement a given number of times is not all that useful. However, in Pascal any number of statements can be grouped together, using a **BEGIN** and **END**, and treated as a single (compound) statement.

Using this fact we can now rewrite the 'add' program as:

```
PROGRAM add (INPUT,OUTPUT);
VAR count:INTEGER;
    total,number:REAL;
BEGIN
    WRITELN;
    total:=0;
    FOR count:=1 TO 4 DO
        BEGIN READ(number);
            total:=total+number
        END;
    WRITELN;
    WRITE(total)
END.
```

The use of **FOR** in this program is very straightforward. The only difference from the previous example ('loop') is the use of **BEGIN** and **END** to group together the two statements to be repeated. (Notice that the semicolon following the first **END** is used to separate the **FOR** statement from the WRITELN.)

A slightly more useful version of this program can be produced by making the final value in the **FOR** statement an expression:

```
PROGRAM add2 (INPUT,OUTPUT);
VAR count, many:INTEGER;
    total, number:REAL;
BEGIN
    WRITELN;
    total:=0;
    READ(many);
    FOR count:=1 TO many
      DO BEGIN WRITELN;
            READ(number);
            total:=total+number
        END;
    WRITE(total)
END.
```

This version will read in any number of REAL numbers and add them up. Try this program and check that you can use it to add together lists of numbers of various lengths—including zero!

Counting **DOWNTO**

The index variable in a standard **FOR** statement starts at a particular value and works its way up to the final value in steps of one. Each time the statement following the **DO** is repeated the index variable has one added to it until it reaches the finish value. It is sometimes useful to have a **FOR** loop that counts backwards. In this case the index variable has one subtracted from it each time until it reaches the final value. The general form of this type of **FOR** loop is:

FOR integer variable:=start value **DOWNTO** final value
DO any statement

Notice that the only obvious change is the use of **DOWNTO** in place of **TO**. However, because the index variable decreases by one each time, the starting value is normally larger than the finishing value. For example:

FOR i:=10 **DOWNTO** 1 **DO** WRITE(i)

prints out 10,9, . . . 1 in descending order.
    DOWNTO can be used in place of **TO** whenever it is an advantage for the index variable to decrease each time through the loop.

The WHILE statement

Although the **FOR** statement is very useful it is restricted to those cases where we know beforehand the number of times that the statement is to be carried out. By contrast, what do we do if we want a program to add up a series of numbers greater than zero without specifying beforehand how many? The solution lies in the use of the **WHILE** statement:

```
PROGRAM sum3(INPUT,OUTPUT);
VAR number, total:REAL;
BEGIN
        total:=0;
        WRITELN;
        READ(number);
        WHILE number >0
          DO BEGIN total:=total+number;
                   WRITELN;
                   READ(number)
             END;
        WRITE(total)
    END.
```

The **WHILE** statement in this program causes the compound statement to be carried out while the condition 'number >0' is true. The flow of control through the program is as follows. First 'total' is zeroed and 'number' is read in. If 'number' is greater than zero the compound statement following the **WHILE** is carried out. The last instruction in this compound reads in a new value for 'number'. Control is then passed back to the beginning of the **WHILE** statement where the test 'number >0' is again applied. If the test is true then the compound statement is carried out once more. If the test is false then control passes to the next statement following the **WHILE** statement. Notice that the **WHILE** statement consists of everything from the word **WHILE** through to the **END** of the compound statement.

The general form of the **WHILE** statement is very simple:

WHILE condition **DO** statement

The statement following the **DO** may be any valid Pascal statement and may of course be a compound statement. The condition following the **WHILE** statement may take many forms but it is always something that can be determined to be true or false. If the condition is true then the statement following the **DO** is carried out. If the condition is false then control passes to the next statement following the **WHILE**. If the statement following the **DO** is carried out, then control always passes to the beginning of the **WHILE** statement.

There are two things to notice about **WHILE** statements. First, the condition may be false the first time that the **WHILE** is executed and in this case the statement following the **DO** is never carried out. Second, the statement must produce a change in the truth of the condition otherwise the **WHILE** statement will never come to an end.

This brings us to the question of the sorts of conditions that are allowed in Pascal. This is such an important topic that it deserves a section all to itself.

Conditional expressions

There are a number of places in Pascal where it is necessary to test if some condition is satisfied or not. For example, in the program illustrating the use of the **WHILE** statement, the condition 'number >0' was used to decide if the **WHILE** was completed or not. It is useful to think of such things as 'number >0' as expressions that evaluate to one of two values, true or false. In this way you can avoid the trap of thinking that 'number >0' is an assertion that what is stored in the variable number *is* greater than zero. If the value stored in 'number' is greater than zero, then 'number >0' is true. If the value stored in 'number' is less than or equal to zero then 'number >0' is false. The general form of a conditional expression is:

expression   relop   expression

where expression is any valid INTEGER or REAL expression and relop is a relational operator. The relational operators allowed in standard Pascal are:

=	equal
<	smaller than
>	greater than
=<	smaller than or equal to
>=	greater than or equal to
<>	not equal

Some examples of simple conditional expressions are:

number1=number 2	is true if the two variables contain the same data
max>min	is true if 'max' is larger than 'min'
max=<min	is true if 'max' is smaller than or equal to 'min'
number1<>number 2	is true if 'number1' is different from 'number2'

Conditional expressions can be a little more complicated; for example:

count+1>large	is true if 'count+1' is bigger than 'large'
num **MOD** 2 = 0	is true if 'num' is divisible by two (i.e. if the remainder is zero)

Notice the difference between a:=b and a=b. The first is an assignment statement which takes the content of variable b and stores it in variable a. The second is a conditional expression, which evaluates to either true or false but does *not* change in any way the contents of a or b. This difference is the reason that Pascal uses the symbol := for assignment where many other languages use = for both purposes.

The problem of order of evaluation exists for relational expressions as well as for arithmetic. In this case it is easily solved because an expression like

36

$$3+count>start*2$$

has only one reasonable interpretation, which is

$$(3+count)>(start*2)$$

because

$$3+ (count)>(start)*2$$

is nonsense. To force the first interpretation in all cases without the use of brackets Pascal assigns the lowest possible priority to any relational operators. This forces all other operations to be carried out *before* any comparisons are made.

The IF statement

We have looked at two ways of carrying out a statement repeatedly but this doesn't cover the possibility that we might want to carry out one of two *different* actions. Selecting one of two different statements can be done by use of the **IF** statement. For example:

```
PROGRAM addsign(INPUT,OUTPUT);
VAR pos,neg,number:REAL;
BEGIN
        pos:=0;neg=0;
        READ(number);
        IF number>0 THEN pos:=pos+1 ELSE neg:=neg+1
END.
```

This program reads in a number and then either adds one to 'pos' or adds one to 'neg'. The flow of control through the program should be fairly obvious from the way it reads. When the **IF** statement is carried out the condition 'number>0' is evaluated: if it is true then the statement following the **THEN** is carried out; if it is false the statement following the **ELSE** is carried out. Notice that only *one* of the two possible statements will be carried out and control then passes to the statement following the **IF**. Of course this program isn't of much use as it stands because it doesn't print any results and only reads in one number but it does show the basic idea behind the **IF** statement.

The general form of the **IF** statement is,

IF condition **THEN** statement1 **ELSE** statement2

where 'condition' is a conditional expression and 'statement1' and 'statement2' are any valid Pascal statements or compound statements. If the condition evaluates to true then 'statement1' is executed otherwise 'statement2' is carried out. Only one of the two statements will be executed and then control passes to the statement following the **IF** statement.

This may sound very easy, and indeed it is, but there are a few complications that we will deal with later. One of the biggest problems that beginners have with **IF** statements is working out where they end. As long as 'statement1' and 'statement2' are simple statements then the end of the **IF** statement is easy to find; if it's not the last statement in the program simply look for the next semicolon. If 'statement1' and 'statement2' are compound statements then things are not quite so easy. For example:

> **IF** a< 0 **THEN BEGIN** a:=a+1;total:=total+a **END**
>   **ELSE BEGIN** a:=a−1;total:=total−a **END;**

There are a number of semicolons separating the statements between the **BEGIN** and **END** so there is no point in looking for the first semicolon as the end of the **IF** statement. The simplest way to find the end of the **IF** statement in this case may seem to be to locate the **END** of the compound statement following the **ELSE**. The trouble with this solution is that there could be something like a **FOR** loop with its own **BEGIN** and **END** inside the compound statement.

The only sure way of finding the end of an **IF** is to read the program carefully. In the example given above the layout, with the **THEN** and **ELSE** on different lines, is very helpful in finding the end of the **IF**. When the compound statements are longer than one line then this layout is not quite so effective but it is still possible to use indentation to show the reader where the **THEN** and **ELSE** parts are. Remember, when you write the program you know where the end of an **IF** statement is; when you read it you have to find it. Anything that you can do with layout to help make the structure of your program clear will be welcomed by any future reader—including yourself!

One-statement **IF**

There is a special case of the general **IF** that is worth considering on its own. Instead of wanting to select which one of two statements is to be carried out, suppose that we have a single statement that is either to be carried out or skipped. For example, in

> **IF** a<0 **THEN** a:=−a **ELSE** a:=a

all that we are trying to do is to make the variable 'a' positive. The statement following the **ELSE** is there just for completeness; it is in fact quite unnecessary. What we really want to say is: if 'a' is smaller than zero then change its sign, otherwise leave it unchanged and get on with the rest of the program. Pascal allows you to say this as:

IF a<0 **THEN** a:=−a

This is a valid second form of the **IF** statement. In general, the one-statement **IF** takes the form:

IF condition **THEN** statement

If the condition evaluates to true then the statement following the **THEN** is carried out and control passes to the next statement. If the condition evaluates to false then control passes directly to the next statement, i.e. the statement following the **THEN** is skipped.

Nesting

Each of the three control statements—**FOR**, **WHILE** and **IF**—are valid Pascal statements. This may seem to be an obvious and un-important observation. However, because each of their respective definitions allow any Pascal statement to be used in the statement part, you can write things like:

IF a<0 **THEN** **IF** b>0 **THEN** a:=a+1 **ELSE** a:=a−1; **ELSE** a:=a+2

or

FOR i:=1 **TO** 10 **DO FOR** j:=1 **TO** 10 **DO** k:=i*j

This inclusion of one control statement inside another is known as nesting. The first example is a nested **IF** and the second is a nested **FOR**.

Nesting is the principal way that complex programs are built up from the very simple control structures that we have. You may feel that the two examples are almost impossible to read, let alone understand! However, if we write the first example in a way that displays its meaning.

    IF a<0 **THEN**
                IF b>0 **THEN** a:=a+1
                  ELSE a:=a−1;
        ELSE a:=a+2;

you should be able to work out what the flow of control is.

The first condition 'a<0' decides which of the **THEN** or **ELSE** parts of the first **IF** will be executed. If it is true then the statement following the **THEN** is carried out. This is another **IF** statement with two parts of its own. If the condition 'b>0' is true then one is added to 'a', otherwise one is subtracted from 'a', and in either case control passes to the statement following the first **IF** statement (i.e. one not shown in the example).

If the first **IF**'s condition evaluates to be false then the statement following the **ELSE** that is written under the first **THEN** is executed. This simply adds two to 'a' and then control passes to the statement following the first **IF**—i.e. in this case the second **IF** statement is never even considered for execution. This should convince you that layout is very important if you want your programs to be readable.

The second example—the nested **FOR**s—can be improved in the same way by layout, though not quite to the same extent:

```
FOR i:=1 TO 10 DO
        FOR j:=1 TO 10 DO
            k:=i*j;
```

The flow of control is such that the first **FOR** causes the second **FOR** to be carried out ten times. Each time the second **FOR** is carried out it causes the statement following its **DO**, i.e. 'k:=i*j', to be carried out ten times. You should be able to work out that this means that 'k:=i*j' is carried out 100 times.

Slightly more difficult is the task of working out what values 'i', 'j' and 'k' take. The first time that the second **DO** is carried out 'i' is 1. The second **FOR** produces values of 'j' from 1 to 10 while 'i' is 1 so the sequence of values is:

i	j	k
1	1	1
1	2	2
1	3	3
.	.	.
.	.	.
.	.	.
1	10	10

When the second **FOR** is complete the first **FOR** adds one to 'i' and then carries out the second **FOR** again, producing the following sequence of values:

i	j	k
2	1	2
2	2	4
2	3	6

$$\begin{array}{ccc} \cdot & \cdot & \cdot \\ \cdot & \cdot & \cdot \\ \cdot & \cdot & \cdot \end{array}$$

2   10   20

You should be able to complete the sequence all the way to the end of the first **FOR** statement i.e. i=10, j=10 and k=100. If you would rather see your computer do all the hard work then try:

```
PROGRAM nest1(INPUT,OUTPUT);
VAR i,j,k :INTEGER;
BEGIN
        FOR i:= 1 TO 10 DO
          FOR j:=1 TO 10 DO
              BEGIN k:=i*j;WRITELN;WRITE(k) END
    END.
```

As you learn to program you will acquire a standard list of often-used nested statements. It is this familiarity with standard forms of the language that separates a beginner from an expert. However, there is only one way to gain such familiarity and that is to write programs!

Two common loops

Programming would be very easy (boring?) if it were possible to provide a catalogue of loops and **IF**s from which any program could be constructed. There are one or two very simple cases that are worth looking at. The first is the sum loop. If you want to add together a collection of numbers then an easy method to use is something like:

```
total:=0;
FOR i:=1 TO amount DO
  BEGIN
    READ(number);total:=total+number
  END
```

This will add 'amount' numbers together keeping a running sum in the variable 'total'. An important point to notice is that 'total' is zeroed before the loop.

The second is the product loop. A less common requirement is to multiply a collection of numbers together. This can be done using something like:

```
prod:=1;
FOR i:=1 TO amount DO
```

BEGIN
        READ(number);prod:=prod*number
    END

which will multiply together 'amount' of numbers keeping a running product in 'prod'. Notice that in this case 'prod' is initialised to one before the loop.

Using nested IFs

The number of possible ways of using nested **IF** statements is too large to list. However, a very common situation is the need to make a choice between more than two statements according to some condition. Suppose that we want to add 1, 2 or 3 to a variable depending on whether another variable is positive, zero or negative. One solution is:

    count:=0;
    IF number>0 **THEN** count:=count+1
                ELSE IF number=0 **THEN** count:=count+2
                            ELSE count:=count+3;
    WRITE(count)

If 'number' is positive then one is added to 'count' and control passes to the WRITE. If 'number' isn't positive then it must be zero or negative and the second **IF** statement is executed. This tests if 'number' is zero and adds two to 'count' if it is. If 'number' isn't zero then it must be negative and the **ELSE** part of the second **IF** statement is executed adding three to 'count'.

This short example illustrates the guideline that it is normally better to nest **IF** statements after the **ELSE** rather than the **THEN** part. The reason for this is that it makes it easier to work out under what overall condition a statement will be executed. If you nest **IF**s only in the **ELSE** parts then the second **IF** will only be carried out if the condition in the first **IF** is false, and so on. So in the above example the last **ELSE** will only be carried out if 'number' is not greater than zero and not equal to zero.

There is one case of nested **IF**s that deserves closer inspection. The nesting,

    IF condition **THEN IF** condition
                THEN statement
                ELSE statement

looks innocent enough, but which **IF** does the **ELSE** belong to? Is the first or second **IF** a single-statement **IF**? The problem is resolved by imposing a rule that **ELSE** is always matched up with the closest **IF**. So the above example is interpreted as:

IF condition **THEN**
        BEGIN IF condition **THEN** statement
               ELSE statement
       END

The CASE statement

In the last section we discovered that by nesting **IF** statements it is possible to select not just one of two options but one of a number. Nested **IF** statements are not always easy to understand and Pascal provides an alternative way of selecting one of a number of alternatives—the **CASE** statement. The general form of the **CASE** statement is

CASE integervariable **OF**
        constantlist:statement;
        constantlist:statement;

        .   .   .

        constantlist:statement
        END

where 'constantlist' is a list of INTEGER constants separated by commas and the 'statement' following the colon may (as usual) be a compound statement. Only one of the list of statements is carried out and then control passes to the statement following the **CASE** statement, i.e. after the **END**. Which statement is carried out depends on the value of the 'integervariable'. The statement corresponding to the 'constantlist' that contains the current value of 'integervariable' is the one carried out. If the current value is not in any of the 'constantlist's then the program stops and an error is reported.

For example:

CASE i **OF**
        2,3:tax:=5;
        1,4:tax:=3
      END

If 'i' (an INTEGER variable) is either 2 or 3 then the statement 'tax:=5' is carried out. If 'i' is 1 or 4 then the statement 'tax:=3' is carried out. If 'i' is any other value then an error is reported and the program stops.

Notice that the numerical values of the constants play no part in the selection process—they act simply as labels and are matched with the current value of the variable. It is obvious that you cannot have the same constant appearing in two lists because of the resulting confusion over which statement should be carried out.

A more realistic example of the use of a **CASE** statement is:

```
READ(taxcat);
CASE  taxcat OF
            1:rate:=0.3;
            2:rate:=0.6;
            3:rate:=0.9
      END
```

This program fragment reads in 'taxcat' which is used to indicate which of three tax categories someone is in and then the **CASE** statement is used to assign the correct tax rate to the variable 'rate'.

Summary

In this chapter we have examined the ideas behind the flow of control and the statements **FOR, WHILE, IF** and **CASE** that can be used to alter it. The **FOR** loop can be used to repeat a statement a known number of times and **WHILE** can be used to repeat a statement until some condition is satisfied. Two forms of the **IF** statement have been introduced. The first takes the form **IF** . . . **THEN** . . . **ELSE** and is used to select one of two statements; the second takes the simpler form **IF** . . . **THEN** . . . and is used to carry out or skip a single statement. As an alternative to using a number of **IF**s the **CASE** statement was introduced to select one of a number of statements.

The idea of a conditional expression was introduced as another example of an expression—in this case evaluating to true or false. The idea of nesting was also introduced, two common program loops—the sum and product loops—were discussed and a common use of nested **IF**s was introduced.

Questions

1. Write a program that will read in 10 numbers and print out their sum and product.

2. Which of the following conditional expressions are true (assuming a:=5;b:=3)?

3+2>2*3
a=b
a<>b
2*a<>6
2*a>=10

3. Write a nested **IF** that carries out the same job as the final example of the **CASE** statement involving 'taxcat'.

4. It is possible to write any **FOR** statement as an equivalent **WHILE**. Can you change

FOR i:=1 to n **DO** WRITE(i)

into an equivalent **WHILE** loop?

5
Pascal in practice

In this chapter we will see how Pascal is used to produce complete programs. There is no doubt that the only way to learn programming is to write programs, yet it is difficult to go from an understanding of the rudiments of a language to writing complete programs without making many mistakes. It is important that, rather than simply reading this chapter and its example programs, you try to write your own. Read the statement of the problem and try to write a program to solve it. If you get stuck then look at the answer following the question but only read as much as you need to carry on—use the text to get 'unstuck'! If you finish the problem without needing to read the solution then compare your program with the one supplied. Try to find out why there are any differences and do not assume that 'the book' is always the best way of doing things. Read the explanations to find out why things are done in a particular way and decide if your way is better.

If you find that you are having a lot of trouble then don't give up straight away and don't start reading the book from the beginning again. Instead try to identify where your difficulty lies. It could be that you haven't understood some key concept such as a variable or flow of control. If so, go back to the appropriate section and, having sorted out the specific problem, try again. It could also be that you understand Pascal but fail to understand the problem that the program is trying to solve. This is a very common difficulty—programmers are always being asked to produce solutions to problems that are outside their knowledge. If this is the case move on to another example.

Example 1—Annual interest

The problem is to calculate the final amount of interest earned by a regular saving plan. Let us suppose that a bank pays interest on the amount deposited only once every year and a saver deposits a fixed amount of money every month. The program should ask for the amount deposited each month and the number of months that the saving will continue for. The output need only be the total sum of money accumulated, including interest earned over the time. For the sake of simplicity assume that the interest rate is fixed at 10 per cent per annum but try to allow for possible future changes in interest rate in your program. Do not use a standard formula for compound interest but try to reproduce the calculation that the bank would do at the end of each year and repeat it for the number of years required.

The solution

Getting started is always the hardest part of any task and programming is no exception. However, there are a few things that are fixed about any program that we are ever going to write. For instance, every one will have a definition section and an instruction section.

In all the examples that we have looked at so far the definition section has been a list of variable names and data types giving no idea of how the variable names and types were arrived at. The answer is that the definitions were constructed with hindsight. As the instruction section of the program takes shape the variables and constants needed are added to the definition section. Any tidying up happens after the program is complete. The best method of constructing the instruction section is to write down a rough solution—not necessarily all in Pascal—and then to produce new versions as each part is changed from a loose description to precise Pascal.

For example, for the first attempt at the program, we might write:

```
PROGRAM interest(INPUT,OUTPUT);
definition section
BEGIN
        read in amount saved per month
        and the time it is to be saved for
        calculate money saved over time, and interest
        write out total amount of money
END.
```

This may not seem like much but it is a big step forward; we have something written down and something to work on—something to refine into a finished program.

The first and last steps in the rough program should be easy to turn into Pascal. To read in the amount and time we need two variables and we might as well call them 'amount' and 'time' but what type should they be? The amount of money could be something like

£20.50 per month so 'amount' should be REAL. You could use an INTEGER variable for 'amount' if you want to add the extra restriction that the money saved must be a whole number of pounds, but this seems unnecessary when using a REAL is so easy. The time of saving should be a whole number of years however because a part year would earn no interest. This means that the variable time should be an INTEGER. The result of the calculation will be the total amount of money in the bank at the end of the time period. A reasonable name for this variable is 'total' and as it will be calculated from 'amount', a REAL variable, it too should be REAL. We can now write a second attempt at the program:

```
PROGRAM interest(INPUT,OUTPUT);
VAR amount,total : REAL;
        time : INTEGER;
BEGIN
        WRITELN;
        READ(amount);WRITELN;READ(time);
        calculate interest and total amount
        WRITE(total)
END.
```

It is now only the middle section that keeps us from our finished program. We could try to convert this section into Pascal in one go. Alternatively, we could first try to arrive at a more detailed English description as follows.

If we know the amount in the bank at the end of a year we can easily calculate the interest earned that year by

interest = amount in bank * interest rate

This interest is added to the bank account so the new total amount in the bank will be

new amount in bank = amount in bank + interest

If we repeat this calculation for each year that the money is saved we have the answer. But we have forgotten to allow for the amount added to the total in the bank as a result of saving. After one year the amount saved is '12*amount per month'. So finally we end up with the following calculations, which will give us the amount in the bank after each year's interest and saving:

amount in the bank this year = amount in bank + yearly savings
                                                last year
interest due   = amount in bank * interest rate
total amount in bank   = amount in bank + interest due
                                                before interest

This description is almost in Pascal already. All we need to do is produce some named variables. The next step towards the final program is:

```
PROGRAM interest(INPUT,OUTPUT);
CONST rate=0.1;
VAR amount,total,interest :REAL;
      time :INTEGER;
BEGIN
      WRITELN;
        READ(amount);WRITELN;READ(time);
        total:=0;
```

Carry out the calculation (below) of amount in bank at the end of each year for 'time' years starting with zero in bank.

```
        BEGIN
        total:=total+12*amount;
        interest:=total*rate;
        total:=total+interest
      END;
        WRITELN;
        WRITE(total)
END.
```

Notice the use of the named constant, 'rate', which makes changing the program to work with different interest rates merely a matter of changing one statement. The compound statement in the middle of the program will work out the amount in the bank at the end of each year's saving. The last step in the production of a finished program is to repeat the calculation for the number of years that saving will continue. This can be done most easily by replacing the written description by a **FOR** statement. The final program is:

```
PROGRAM interest(INPUT,OUTPUT);
CONST rate=0.1
VAR amount,total,interest:REAL;
      time,i:INTEGER;
BEGIN
      WRITELN;
        READ(amount);WRITELN;READ(time);
        total:=0;
        FOR i:=1 TO time DO
          BEGIN
                total:=total+12*amount;
                interest:=total*rate;
                total:=total+interest
        END;
```

            WRITELN;
            WRITE(total)
    END.

At this point you have arrived at a program that you can run and test on a computer. Frequently there will be some unforeseen error present; often a variable will have been used but not defined. Run your version of the program and note any errors, correct them and run the program again. Carry on like this until you have a program that works to your satisfaction.

You could improve this program immeasurably by printing out intermediate results and checking for silly inputs such as a negative 'amount' or 'time' but all of these improvements can be seen as continuing the refinement process started with the first rough program. In this sense no program is ever finished; you simply reach a level of refinement beyond which it is not worth going!

Example 2—Factorials

This program will calculate the factorial of a number. The input is a single integer, n say, and the output is the factorial (usually represented by n!):

$$n*(n-1)*(n-2)*(n-3) \ldots . 1$$

For example, if n is 5 then 5! is

$$5*4*3*2*1 \text{ i.e. } 120$$

Include facilities in your program to check the validity of the input; that is, check to ensure that it is positive.

The solution

Proceeding as with the first example, a rough solution is

    PROGRAM fac(INPUT,OUTPUT);
    definition section
    BEGIN
            input number
            calculate factorial
            print result
    END.

The refinement of the 'input number' and 'print result' parts is fairly easy once we have settled on a name such as 'number' for the input

variable and 'answer' for the output variable; both are obviously
INTEGER. The 'calculate factorial' part is the core of the program
and can be written by examining the definition of the factorial.
Factorial n is the product of the collection of numbers between 1 and
n. We can produce the numbers between 1 and n with a **FOR** statement and from there obtaining their product is straightforward.

```
PROGRAM fac(INPUT,OUTPUT);
VAR number,answer,i :INTEGER;
BEGIN
        WRITELN;
        READ(number);
        answer:=1;
        FOR i:=1 TO number DO answer:=answer*i;
        WRITELN;
        WRITE(answer)
END.
```

Notice that because there is only one statement following the **DO**
there is no need to use a **BEGIN** and **END** in the **FOR** statement.
This is a finished program in the sense that it calculates factorials,
but it isn't complete according to our earlier specification because it
does nothing about checking the input data. It should be obvious
that what we have to add is a test to make sure that 'number' is greater
than zero. If it is, then the program should be carried out as it stands
and if it isn't then the program should end.

```
PROGRAM fac(INPUT,OUTPUT);
VAR number,answer,i :INTEGER;
BEGIN
        WRITELN;
        READ(number);
        IF number>0 THEN BEGIN
                        answer :=1;
                        FOR  i:=1  TO  number  DO
                            answer:=answer*1;
                        WRITELN;
                        WRITE(answer)
                      END
END.
```

This final version of the program should be studied until you are
sure that you understand the flow of control through the program in
the case of 'number'>0 and 'number'=<0. Notice that the single-
statement form of the **IF** is sufficient here because we either want to
carry out the rest of the program or do nothing. In a more sophisti-

cated version of the program it would be better to print an error message, telling the user that the input has to be positive rather than just stopping the program. This would use an

IF . . THEN do program **ELSE** print error

form of the **IF** but, as we have not yet examined how to print messages of any sort, this will have to wait.

Comments

As we have been constructing programs, all of the incidental information concerning them has been recorded in the text. For example in the interest program it was necessary to say that 'rate' was a constant that could be changed to apply different interest rates. It would obviously be an advantage if such information could be incorporated into the program in some way. Pascal allows this via the comment statement.

You can insert any information of any sort in a program without affecting its meaning as long as it is surrounded by either (* and *) or { and }. You cannot mix the type of brackets; if you start a comment with (* then you must finish it with *). For example, in the case of the interest program we could add a line before or after the **CONST** statement like:

(*   Rate is the current interest rate and may be changed   *)

This information can be read by any future user and does not change the meaning of the program in any way. Your computer will not even examine what is in between comment brackets; it takes the attitude that comments are for the user only!

Apart from this basic use of comments to include information about modifying programs, it is a good idea to add comments that explain how a program works. For the simple programs that we have written so far, comments have been unnecessary because the programs have been so short that their meaning should be clear from reading. With longer programs this ceases to be the case and if you are to have any hope of returning to a program after some time and understanding how it works you *must* add comments as you write it.

Example 3—Mean and variance

The problem that this program has to solve is the calculation of the mean and variance of a set of numbers. If there are N numbers in the set then the mean is simply their sum divided by N. The variance is a little more difficult and the method is to:

1. Work out the sum of all the numbers . . . call this 'sum'.
2. Work out the sum of all the *squares* of the numbers . . . call this 'sumsq'.
3. The variance is then given by:

$$\frac{(\text{sumsq}-\text{sum}*\text{sum}/N)}{N}$$

These steps almost tell you how to write the program!

The first rough attempt is:

```
PROGRAM stat(INPUT,OUTPUT);
VAR sum,sumsq:REAL;
        n:INTEGER;
BEGIN
        (* read in data and calculate sum,sumsq and n *)
        (* using sum,sumsq and n calculate the mean and
        variance*)
        (* printout mean and variance*)
END.
```

As we are becoming more sophisticated the first rough program contains more information than previous examples. The English descriptions are now enclosed in comment brackets and this means that they can be left in the finished program as descriptions of how it works—they now serve two purposes.

Before we can move on to a refinement of the program we must decide how to read in the collection of values that forms the data. We could ask for the number of values to be entered before the input of the first data value or we could use a particular data value (-9999 say) to indicate the end of the data. Using the first method is easier:

```
PROGRAM stat(INPUT,OUTPUT);
VAR sum,sumsq,mean,var,number:REAL;
      n,i:INTEGER;
BEGIN
    WRITELN;
    READ(n); (*read number of data values*)
    (* read in data and calculate sum and sumsq*)
    sum:=0;sumsq:=0; (*initialise variables to zero *)
    FOR i:=1 TO n DO
```

```
        BEGIN
            WRITELN;
            READ(number); (* read data *)
            sum:=sum+number; (* add to sum *)
            sumsq:=sumsq+number*number
                        (* add square of number to sumsq *)
        END;
    (* calculate mean and variance *)
    mean:=sum/n;
    var:=(sumsq-sum*sum/n)/n;
    (* print results *)
    WRITELN;
    WRITE(mean);
    WRITELN;
    WRITE(var)
END.
```

This last refinement is in fact the final version of the program. As you become more confident then the refinement process can be speeded up by working on more than one part of the program at a time. Notice the use of brackets to make the meaning of the expressions clear.

Summary

In this chapter we have looked at how Pascal can be used to solve three simple problems. The method of stepwise refinement was introduced in the way each example was solved. The idea and importance of the Pascal comment was also discussed.

Questions

1. Change the interest rate in program 'interest' to 20 per cent per annum.

2. Add an **IF** statement to the program 'interest' to reject negative savings!

3. Change the program 'interest' so that it prints out total amount saved and the total interest earned.

6

Functions and procedures

We have already one method of building new instructions from old—the compound statement. In this chapter we examine two other ways of extending the range of things that we can easily use to construct complex programs—functions and procedures.

Functions

A function is an operation on data that results in a single answer. This definition may seem very vague but this reflects the wide range of operations that constitute functions; their unifying feature is that they all produce a single data value as their result. The most common examples of functions come from mathematics. For example, the sine of an angle is a function; you specify an angle and the result is a single number (between -1 and 1) that is its sine. Another example is the square root of a number, or less obviously, the maximum of a set of five numbers.

The importance of the fact that functions return only single answers is that this enables them to be written on the right-hand side of an assignment statement or be combined together in expressions. The usual notation for a function involves giving it a name, e.g. SIN for sine and SQRT for square root, and writing the data that it will operate on in brackets to the right of the name. Thus:

SIN(theta) means the sine of the angle 'theta'
SQRT(number) means the square root of 'number'

The number or variable that appears inside the brackets is called the parameter of the function. As mentioned earlier, in Pascal a function can be used in any expression or assignment statement. For example:

ans:=SQRT(number)+5

Not only can a function be used in an expression but its parameter can be an expression, for example:

ans:=SQRT(2*2)+5

Indeed the parameter can be an expression that involves another, possibly the same, function. For example:

ans:=SQRT(2*SQRT(2)+5)+10

Although there is the absolute restriction on the number of answers that a function may return there is no such restriction on the number of parameters a function may have. For example, if we have a function that returns the maximum of five numbers then it needs five separate parameters. These are written separated by commas thus:

ans:=max(a,b,c,d,e)

As you can see, the function notation is a very powerful way of extending the range of expressions available.

Functions in Pascal

Pascal recognises two types of function—supplied functions and ones that are user-defined. There are some functions that are used so often that they have been built into the language as standard. These are the supplied functions and they are freely available for use. Any functions that are not supplied by the language must be defined by the user. Apart from the need to define a user-defined function they can be used in the same way as supplied functions. Because of this we will look at supplied functions and their use and then consider the way that Pascal allows new functions to be defined.

The first thing to notice about functions is that they return data that will be of a specific type. This type must be correct for the sort of expression that the function will be used in, or for the variable that the result will be assigned to. The type of the data that a function returns is normally called the type of the function. For example, Pascal supplies the REAL function SIN. This means that for all practical purposes the function SIN must be treated as if it was a REAL variable. Thus the expression:

ans:=SIN(x)

is only valid if ans is a REAL variable. Not only do we have to consider the type of the answer that a function returns but we also have to consider the type of the parameter(s) that can be used.

A list of the standard supplied Pascal functions is given below. Notice that for the sake of completeness some of the functions listed return and use data types that have not yet been defined. These

56

functions will be discussed in more detail when their data types are discussed later in the book. Some of the supplied functions allow the additional freedom of using one or two data types as parameters in which case the result is taken to be of the same type as the parameter itself. For example, the function ABS, which finds the absolute value of a number, can be used either as an INTEGER or a REAL function: i.e. ABS(x) will be REAL if x is REAL and INTEGER if x is INTEGER. This avoids the need to have two ABS functions, one for REAL and one for INTEGER, but it should be noted that this facility does not extend to user-defined functions, which are always of a fixed type.

Standard supplied functions

Name	Description	Type of parameter	Type of result
	Arithmetic functions		
ABS(x)	absolute value of x i.e. x if x is +ve and −x if x is −ve	REAL/INTEGER	same as type of parameter
SQR(x)	square of x i.e. x*x	REAL/INTEGER	same as type of parameter
SIN(x)	sine of x (x must be in radians not degrees)	REAL/INTEGER	REAL
COS(x)	cosine of x (x must be in radians not degrees)	REAL/INTEGER	REAL
EXP(x)	e raised to the power x	REAL/INTEGER	REAL
LN(x)	natural logarithm	REAL/INTEGER	REAL
SQRT(x)	square root of x	REAL/INTEGER	REAL
ARCTAN(x)	gives the angle, in radians, whose TAN is x	REAL/INTEGER	REAL
	Predicate functions		
ODD(x)	TRUE if x is odd	INTEGER	BOOLEAN
EOF(f)	TRUE if at the end of file f	string	BOOLEAN
EOLN(f)	TRUE if at the end of a line of text file f	string	BOOLEAN
	Transfer functions		
TRUNC(x)	converts x into an integer by chopping off the fractional part	REAL	INTEGER
ROUND(x)	converts x into an integer by rounding	REAL	INTEGER
ORD(x)	the ordinal number of x	various	INTEGER
CHR(x)	the character, if there is one, whose ordinal number is x	INTEGER	CHAR
	Ordering functions		
SUCC(x)	the successor of x	various	same as parameter
PRED(x)	the predecessor of x	various	same as parameter

Even from this long list, the functions PACK, UNPACK, NEW and DISPOSE have been left out. The reason for this omission is that different Pascals treat them in different ways and consideration of them is best left until later. The functions listed above are the ones that you can normally expect to find in any Pascal implementation—there may be extras in specific versions and the best way to find out about these is to read your manual. However, if you can keep to the functions listed above you can be fairly sure that any programs that you write will run on any machine.

An example—Quadratic equation

As an example of a program that uses supplied functions consider the problem of finding the solution to a quadratic equation using the standard school book formula:

$$\text{root1} = \frac{-b + \text{SQRT}(\text{discriminant})}{2a}$$

$$\text{root2} = \frac{-b - \text{SQRT}(\text{discriminant})}{2a}$$

where discriminant = b*b − 4*a*c
and the equation is:

$$ax^2 + bx + c = 0$$

There are real solutions if you can take the square root of the discriminant and this is only possible if the discriminant is non-negative (i.e. positive or zero).

The resulting program is:

```
PROGRAM root(INPUT,OUTPUT);
VAR a,b,c,root1,root2,disc:REAL;
BEGIN
    WRITELN;
    READ(a); (* read in coefficients*)
    WRITELN;READ(b);
    WRITELN;READ(c);
    disc:=SQR(b)-4*a*c; (* calculate discriminant *)
    IF disc>=0 THEN BEGIN
                        (* if discriminant +ve or zero *)
                        root1:=(-b+SQRT(disc))/2*a;
                        root2:=(-b-SQRT(disc))/2*a;
                        WRITE(root1);WRITE(root2)
                    END
END.
```

User-defined functions

A user-defined function must be defined BEFORE its first use. After all the usual **VAR** and **CONST** statements in the definition part of the program you can define as many different functions as you want to use in the instruction part of the program. Each function is defined by a function heading of the form:

FUNCTION identifier (parameter list): result type

Where the 'identifier' is the name of the function and the 'parameter list' is a list in the style of a **VAR** statement of variable names and types. The form of the parameter list can be quite complicated. The 'result type' is, as its name suggests, simply the type of the single value that the function returns. An example of a function definition is:

FUNCTION max(a,b:REAL):REAL

which defines the function 'max' to be a REAL function with two REAL parameters. Following the function heading is a list of Pascal statements that essentially take the form of a Pascal program. It has its own definition section and its own instruction section. For example, if the function 'max' finds the maximum value of two numbers it must be defined as follows:

```
FUNCTION max(a,b:REAL):REAL;
VAR temp:REAL;
BEGIN
        IF a>b THEN temp:=a ELSE temp:=b;
        max:=temp
END
```

Notice that if you replaced the **FUNCTION** statement by a **PROGRAM** statement there would be no difference between this user-defined function and a program. You can look on a function as a program that can be used by another program! The names given to the parameters, i.e. 'a' and 'b', are not very important in the sense that they are only used in the instruction part of the function to show what happens to the first parameter, the second, and so on. You could read the program something like 'if the first parameter is greater than the second parameter . . .' and so on.

It is important to distinguish between the parameters used to define the function—i.e. 'a' and 'b' in this case—and the real parameters that you would write when *using* the function, for example 'max(2,3)'. The parameters that are used to define the function are often called formal parameters. The last but one line of the function should indicate to you how the answer is associated with the function. The value of 'temp' is assigned to the name of the function and this is the value that the function returns in an assignment statement.

Once defined, a user function can be used in the same way as a supplied function. For example, if the definition of the 'max' function is included in a program to find the maximum of two numbers, all we have to do is write:

```
ans:=max(3.4,5.6); (* would assign 5.6 to ans *)
ans:=max(number1,number2); (* would assign the larger to ans *)
```

As you would expect from a consideration of the use of supplied functions, the names that you give to the parameters in the function definition have no bearing on the parameters that you can use with the function.

A short, but complete example of the use of a function may be found in the following program:

```
PROGRAM power(INPUT,OUTPUT);
VAR number,ans:REAL;
     n:INTEGER;
FUNCTION pow(x:REAL;n:INTEGER):REAL;
VAR temp:REAL;
     i:INTEGER;
BEGIN
      temp:=1.0;
      FOR i:=1 TO n DO temp:=temp*x;
      pow:=temp
END;      (* end of function *)
BEGIN (* start of main program *)
      READ(number);READ(n);
      ans:=pow(number,n);
      WRITELN;
      WRITE(ans)
END.
```

This short program will raise any real number to a positive integer power (e.g. it will work out 2.3 raised to the power of 5). The function 'pow' is defined at the start of the program and used later in the body of the program. Notice that both the program and the function have definition sections where they define the variables that they use. The relationship between these variables will be the subject of a later section.

There are a number of complications concerning the naming and use of parameters but it is better to leave a discussion of these until later. However, it is worth noticing that because of the way functions are used the parameters can only be used to pass data *to* the function. For example, if there is an assignment to a parameter within a function only the variable within the function is changed. You can see that this is true if you run the following program:

```
PROGRAM test(INPUT,OUTPUT);
VAR a,b:INTEGER;
FUNCTION mix(p1,p2:INTEGER):INTEGER;
BEGIN
        p1:=1;p2:=2;
        mix:=3
END;
BEGIN
        a:=4;b:=5;
        a:=mix(a,b);
        WRITE(a);WRITE(b)
END.
```

The function assigns 1 and 2 to its first and second parameters and always returns 3 as its result. In the main program, where the function is used, you might expect the values of 'a' and 'b' always to be changed by the parameter assignments in the function—but they are not. The value of 'a' becomes 3 because of the assignment of the function 'mix' to it and 'b' is 5 because it is the subject of an assignment in the main program.

This program shows that *the parameters in a function have nothing to do with any variables in the main program.* All that happens is that when the name of the function is used the value of any parameter is passed to the function to be used. Hence the name of this type of parameter—a value parameter. If you think about it this is the only way it could work if expressions are to be allowed as parameters. For example, 'mix(3+3,4+1)' is a valid use of the function 'mix'. At the start of the function the value of the first expression is passed to the parameter 'p1', i.e. 'p1' is 6 and similarly 'p2' is 5.

Procedures

Functions are very useful but what about the cases when more than one result is produced by an operation—or indeed where no result is returned? It might be possible to split the operation down to the point at which it can be represented by a number of functions; for example, the operation of finding the maximum and the minimum of three numbers could be implemented as two functions, 'max' and 'min'. However, there is sufficient reason to create another way of putting a list of Pascal statements together to create a new single operation. A procedure is the name given to such a collection of statements and Pascal procedures are not restricted to returning a single result.

A Pascal procedure is defined in roughly the same way as a Pascal function. Indeed, most things that are true of functions are true of procedures except that procedures cannot be used in assignment statements or expressions. The **PROCEDURE** statement takes the form:

PROCEDURE identifier(parameter list)

The 'identifier' is the name by which the procedure is known and the 'parameter list' is similar to that introduced for functions but has one extra feature which will be discussed below. Notice that there is no need to define the type of the procedure because there might be more than one result and hence more than one type.

This leaves us the problem of how to return any results from the procedure. In the case of the function, the parameters could only be used to pass values to the function—changing values of the parameters within the function does not affect anything in the main program. To allow procedures to pass results back to the main program we have to use a new type of parameter that allows communication in both directions.

The new sort of parameter is known as a variable parameter and is indicated by writing **VAR** in front of its definition. For example:

PROCEDURE swap(**VAR** a,b:INTEGER);

Notice that the only difference between the previous parameter list and this is the word **VAR** written in front. You can think of a variable parameter as a way of passing a variable from the main program into the procedure whereas our previous use of parameter passed only a value. This is best illustrated by an example:

```
PROGRAM proc1(INPUT,OUTPUT);
VAR a,b,c:INTEGER;
PROCEDURE pass (VAR p1,p2:INTEGER);
BEGIN
        p1:=1;p2:=2
END;
BEGIN
        a:=3;b:=4;
        pass(a,b);
        WRITE(a);WRITE(b)
END.
```

If you run this program you will find that the final values of 'a' and 'b' are 1 and 2 respectively. That is, their values _have_ been changed by the procedure. Because assignment to variable parameters must change the value of a variable in the main program it should be obvious that expressions cannot be passed to procedures. For example in 'pass(3+4,b+2)' there are no variables that can be associated with 'p1' and 'p2'.

Pascal provides some supplied procedures as well as functions. These are not as numerous but are very important. You should now recognise READ and WRITE as procedures that read data into a variable and write data from a variable. We will meet other supplied procedures concerned with input/output in a later chapter.

Value and variable parameters—an overview

We have covered a lot of ground in dealing with functions and procedures and it is now worth summarising and adding to what we have learned about parameters.

When defining functions or procedures we use formal parameters. These are simply identifiers used to show what must be done to the actual parameters when the function or procedure is used. When a function or procedure is used, there must be as many actual parameters as there were formal parameters and they must be of the same type.

There are two sorts of parameter—value and variable parameters. Variable parameters are distinguished from value parameters by the word **VAR** in front of the parameter/type list. E.g. **PROCEDURE (VAR** p1:REAL) defines a variable parameter and **PROCEDURE** (p1:REAL) defines a value parameter.

A formal value parameter may be replaced by an expression of the same type as the actual parameter. The action of a value parameter is such that the value of any variable of expression used as an actual parameter is passed to the corresponding parameter in the function or procedure. This implies that once this has happened there is no association between any variable used as an actual parameter and the parameter in the function, i.e. assignment to the parameter in the function/procedure has no effect on the original variable.

A formal variable parameter must be replaced by a variable of the correct type—replacing it by an expression will cause an error. The action of a variable parameter is different from that of a value parameter in that the variable used as the actual parameter is passed. This can be thought of as the variable used as the actual parameter _becoming_ the parameter in the function or procedure. In other words, assignment to a variable parameter in a function or a procedure does alter the value of the actual parameter in the main program.

When you use a parameter, either in a function or a procedure, you can choose to make it a value or a variable parameter. You can also mix value and variable parameters in the same function or procedure. However, the use of variable parameters in functions is to be avoided because functions should be used in situations when only one result is to be produced. An example of a mixed value/variable procedure is:

PROCEDURE test(**VAR** a,b:INTEGER;c,d:REAL;
VAR e,f:REAL)

This defines 'a' and 'b' to be variable parameters of type INTE-GER, 'c' and 'd' to be value parameters of type REAL and 'e' and 'f' to be variable parameters of type REAL.

Some general guidelines for when to use value and variable parameters are:

1. Never use variable parameters in functions.
2. Use variable parameters in procedures when you want to get results back.
3. Use value parameters in a procedure whenever you do not want to get results back; they allow expressions to be used as actual parameters.

Global and local variables

We have spent some time considering the action of the two different types of parameter but functions and procedures can also define their own variables in their definition section. What relationship, if any, do these variables have to variables defined in the main program or in other functions and procedures?

Any variables that are defined in the main program are available for use by any function or procedure; they are said to be global to the function or procedure. For example:

```
PROGRAM global1(INPUT,OUTPUT);
VAR main1:INTEGER;
PROCEDURE test;
BEGIN
    main1:=main1+1
END;
```

BEGIN
> main1:=0;
> test;
> WRITE(main1)

END.

Notice that although the procedure has no parameters and does not define any variables, it can add one to a variable defined in the main program. Not only that but it is the same variable as the one in the main program, i.e. the procedure changes the value of 'main1' in the main program to from 0 to 1. Procedures or functions that use variables that are defined in the main program are said to produce side-effects. It is good programming practice to avoid side-effects in functions and procedures because it makes it difficult to see what such functions/procedures are doing. It is much better to keep all of the interaction between a function or a procedure and the main program confined to the use of parameters.

Variables defined in a function or a procedure are created for the time that the function or procedure is being carried out and then they are destroyed. This means that they are created afresh every time that you use the function or procedure and cannot be used by the main program. Such variables are called local variables.

The only possibility of confusion arises if we have a global variable and a local variable of the same name. That is, a main program defines a variable, say 'count', and then a function or procedure defines the same variable. The cause of confusion lies in the end of the last sentence because the function or procedure does not define the *same* variable; it defines a *new* variable which just happens to have the same name.

When you are in the main program the main program's variable is available. As soon as you move into the function or procedure a new variable with the same name is created—the local version of the main program's variable. This means that while you are in the function/procedure any reference to the variable will use the local variable and any values stored in the main program's global variable cannot be reached. The global variable still exists and when you go back to the main program its contents will be unchanged; it isn't destroyed, just inaccessible. The subject of who owns a variable and if it's local or global is often called the scope of a variable.

To illustrate the workings of global and local variables consider the following program:

PROGRAM scope(INPUT,OUTPUT);
VAR same,b:INTEGER;
PROCEDURE test;

```
VAR same:INTEGER; (* same is in main program as well *)
BEGIN
        b:=1; (* b is global *)
        same:=2; (* same is local *)
        WRITE(b);WRITE(same)
END;
BEGIN (* main program *)
    b:=4;same:=3; (* both b and same belong to main *)
    test; (* use test *)
    WRITE(b);WRITE(same)
END.
```

In this program there are three variables, the globals 'same' and 'b', and the local variable 'same'. The program starts by setting 'same' and 'b' to 3 and 4 respectively in the main program and then uses the procedure 'test'. This creates a new variable 'same' and then assigns 1 to the global variable 'b' and 2 to the local variable 'same'. Writing both of them out displays 1 and 2. Returning to the main program and once again writing out 'b' and 'same' displays 1 and 3—emphasising that the variable 'same' in the main program and the procedure is identical in name only. The main program's variable 'same' was set to 3 at the start of the program and was not altered again. The procedure 'test' created a new variable 'same' that had 2 stored in it and was then printed out.

Notice that, while in 'test', there is no way of getting at the main program's version of 'same'; using the identifier 'same' is taken to be a reference to the variable created by the procedure. On returning to the main program the procedure's version of 'same' is destroyed and therefore any reference to 'same' returns to meaning the original variable defined by the main program.

This idea of global and local variables is not difficult in theory. A function or procedure has access to all the variables defined in the main program but creates new versions of all variables that it defines. These new versions are destroyed at the end of the function/procedure. However, it can be quite confusing in practice. Having multiple copies of variables with the same name can be a headache for even the most experienced programmer!

Nesting of functions and procedures

Functions and procedures have a definition part and an instruction part. It should come as no surprise that the definition part of a function or a procedure can contain the definition of another function or procedure! In fact a function or a procedure can be treated exactly like a main program and can use all the statements and facilities available to a main program. In Pascal this two-part structure of definitions and instructions is so important that it is given a special name—a block—and Pascal is said to be a block-structured language. Programs, functions and procedures are all examples of blocks and differ only in the form of their heading, namely their **PROGRAM**, **FUNCTION** or **PROCEDURE** statements. Any function or procedure defined in another block is said to be contained in that block.

The only difficulty that this nested structure can cause is working out more general rules of local and global variables. If a block defines a variable then it is local to that block and global to any other block defined *within* the first block. For example:

```
........PROGRAM main;
.           VAR a,b,c:INTEGER;
.
.
.       ......PROCEDURE one;
.       .     VAR c,d,e:INTEGER;
.       .
.       .     ..PROCEDURE two;
.       .     . VAR e,f,g:INTEGER;
.       .     . BEGIN
.       .     .           statements of procedure two
.       .     ..END;
.       .
.       .     BEGIN
.       .               statements of procedure one
.       .....END;
.           BEGIN
.                   statements of main program
........END.
```

The main program defines a procedure called 'one', which defines a procedure called 'two'. The variables 'a', 'b' and 'c' are global to both procedures but 'c' is replaced by a local version in procedure 'one'. The variables 'c', 'd', 'e' are local to procedure 'one' but global to procedure 'two', but 'e' is replaced by a local version in procedure 'two'. If procedure 'two' makes use of 'a' and 'b' then it uses the main program's variables. If it makes use of 'c' then it uses the variable created by procedure 'one'. You can carry on analysing which variable is accessible from which procedure to discover if you understand the ideas of local and global variables by doing the questions at the end of the chapter.

The same rules for global and local apply to all the identifiers used in a program, no matter what they are used for. For example, if a function is defined in a block then it is local to that block, and global to any inner block. This means that it can be used within the defining block and any blocks contained within that block, unless the inner block redefines it. You should recognise this as the same sort of rule that applies to variables.

Using functions and procedures

The idea of functions and procedures is basic to efficient programming. In Chapter 5 the idea of writing a program by refinement was introduced, and functions and procedures can be used to aid this method. If you are writing a rough description of a program you could assume that a procedure exists to solve some part of the problem and just write its name in the main program. You can complete the main program before going back and writing the procedures used. You can extend this use of unwritten procedures to the writing of the procedures, and so on until everything is defined. This method of writing programs is known as top-down design but it is more important that you appreciate how to go about writing programs than remember its name.

Another way that functions and procedures are useful is in making a program more readable. For example, suppose that very early on in a program there are two distinct courses of action to be taken depending upon some condition. That is, the program divides into two at an **IF** statement with many instructions following both the **THEN** and the **ELSE**. A clearer way of showing this is to define two procedures corresponding to the instructions following the **THEN** and the **ELSE** and use

   IF condition **THEN** proc1 **ELSE** proc2

which is very much easier to understand.

There are so many reasons why functions and procedures should be used that it could take up the rest of the book! Suffice it to say that they are well worth mastering.

Summary

In this chapter the ideas of a function and a procedure have been introduced. Two types of parameter have been discussed—value and variable parameters. Global and local variables were also introduced.

Questions

1. Write a program that will print out the square and square root of all the integers between 1 and 20.

2. Use the function 'max' defined earlier in this chapter to find the largest of four numbers.

3. Extend the function 'max' to finding the maximum of three numbers.

4. Write a procedure 'maxmin' that will find the largest and smallest of three numbers.

5. In the example involving 'main', 'one' and 'two': if procedure 'one' assigns values to 'a', 'b', 'c', 'd' and 'e', which variables are changed in the main program?

7
More on data types: BOOLEAN, CHAR, scalar and user-defined types

The number of data types available in Pascal is most certainly one of its strong points. So far the only data types that have been introduced are REAL and INTEGER; both are examples of numeric data. Pascal provides a wide range of non-numeric data types and these form the subject of the first part of this chapter. The second part considers the subject of user-defined types and scalar types in general.

BOOLEAN type

It may come as something of a surprise to discover that we have already met the data type BOOLEAN in an earlier chapter. When we considered conditional expressions the idea that they evaluate to one of two values—true or false—was introduced without discussion. Pascal provides variables of type BOOLEAN to allow the results of conditional expressions to be saved for later use. A BOOLEAN variable is one that can only be used to store one of two values—true or false—and can be defined using the usual **VAR** statement in conjunction with the type identifier BOOLEAN. For cxample:

   VAR ans,cond,yes:BOOLEAN

defines 'ans', 'cond' and 'yes' to be BOOLEAN.

A constant of this type can only be either true or false so the simplest BOOLEAN assignment is:

   ans:=true

or

   ans:=false

We have already used some examples of BOOLEAN expressions in conditional expressions. For example, $2<3$ is an expression that evaluates to true. You can assign the result of a BOOLEAN expression to a BOOLEAN variable thus:

   ans:=2<3

This assignment statement may look a little odd and it sometimes helps to put an unnecessary bracket around the conditional expression:

   ans:= (2<3)

but it's all a matter of taste and both assignment statements result in the value true being stored in the variable 'ans'. A BOOLEAN expression that often strikes beginners as being very odd-looking is:

   ans:= var1=var2

It is probably the double occurrence of the equals sign that causes the trouble. If you read the statement carefully there need be no difficulty. If 'var1' is equal to 'var2' then the value of 'ans' is true, otherwise it is false.

The range of BOOLEAN expressions allowed in Pascal is much greater than simple conditional expressions. There are three BOOLEAN operators, **AND, OR** and **NOT. AND** and **OR** operate on two BOOLEAN variables as * or + operate on two REAL or INTEGER variables. **NOT** operates on a single variable rather like the minus in '$-a$'. The result of the operations is close to the usual English meaning of the terms AND, OR and NOT.

   BOOLEAN expression1 **AND** BOOLEAN expression2

is true if BOTH expressions are true, and false otherwise.

   BOOLEAN expression1 **OR** BOOLEAN expression2

is true if EITHER of the expressions is true, and false only if both expressions are false.

   NOT BOOLEAN expression

is false if the expression is true, and true otherwise.

Some examples should help to make these definitions clear: assuming a:=5;b:=3 then

   (a=5) **AND** (b=3) is true
   (a<0) **AND** (b=3) is false
   (a<0) **OR** (b=3) is true
   NOT (a=5)   is false
   NOT (a=3)   is true

As in the case of arithmetic expressions and the *,+,$-$ operators,

BOOLEAN operators can be combined together to form quite complicated operations. Once again the problem of order of evaluation crops up and is solved by assigning priorities:

Operator   Priority

NOT   3 (highest)
AND   2
OR   1

Any BOOLEAN expression is evaluated starting with the highest priority operator, any ties being resolved by working from left to right. Thus:

NOT a **AND** b

is evaluated as

(**NOT** a) **AND** b

You may be wondering why expressions such as:

(a<b) **AND** (c=3)

have brackets around the relational expressions. For the reason we have to go back to Chapter 4 where it was explained that the relational operators have the lowest possible priorities. If the normal rules of evaluation are applied to

a<b **AND** c=3

then we get

a< (b **AND** c) =3

which, apart from not being what was intended, is nonsense. It pays to remember that relational operators are always worked out last, unless you put brackets around them.

Using BOOLEAN expressions

Although it was stated that a BOOLEAN variable can be used to save the result of a conditional expression, no hint of why you might want to store the result of a BOOLEAN expression has yet been given. The answer lies in the fact that anywhere that you can use a conditional expression you can use a BOOLEAN expression. (This is not unreasonable as a conditional expression is nothing more than a special case of a BOOLEAN expression.) So far we have come across two cases where conditional expressions are used—the

WHILE loop and the **IF** statement. Now that we know about BOO-LEAN expressions we can write statements such as:

IF (a>0) **AND** (b<0) **THEN** ... **ELSE** ...
WHILE (a=0) **OR** (b<0) **DO** ...

which increases the power and range of both statements enormously. Notice that, as a single BOOLEAN variable is just a special case of an expression, the following are also legal if 'yes' and 'ans' are BOOLEAN variables:

IF yes **THEN** ... **ELSE** ...
WHILE ans **DO** ...

The principal use of simple BOOLEAN variables is in passing back conditions in procedures. For example:

```
PROGRAM flag(INPUT,OUTPUT);
VAR a,b,ans:REAL;
     error:BOOLEAN;
PROCEDURE   divide(p1,p2:REAL;VAR   result:REAL;VAR
flag:BOOLEAN);
BEGIN
        flag:=(p2=0);
        IF NOT flag THEN result:=p1/p2
END;
(* start of main program *)
BEGIN
        WRITELN;
        READ(a);READ(b);
        WRITELN;
        divide(a,b,ans,error);
        IF NOT error THEN WRITE(ans)
END.
```

The procedure 'divide' attempts to divide 'p1' by 'p2'. This is impossible if 'p2' is zero so it checks for this condition and only carries out the division if 'p2' is not zero. This is fine, but the main program is going to print the result of the division—what if the division was never carried out? The answer lies in the use of a BOOLEAN variable parameter which passes back the result of the test in the procedure.

This example may seem to be very simple but the general idea is very useful when the procedure is more complicated and the range of error conditions is larger. A BOOLEAN variable, or any other sort of variable used to signal a condition, is often called a flag.

After using BOOLEAN expressions for a while you will find ways
of simplifying expressions to make them easier to read and more
efficient. Some examples of simplifications are:

NOT(**NOT**(a)) = a
NOT(a<b) = a>=b
NOT(a<>b) = a=b
a **AND** (b **OR** c) = a **AND** b **OR** a **AND** c
a **OR** (b **AND** c) = (a **OR** b) **AND** (a **OR** c)

BOOLEAN expressions can often be simplified by common sense
but be careful and check that you have got them right. One of the
most common of simple errors in a program is the mistaken interpretation of a BOOLEAN expression.

Output of BOOLEAN type

Although a full discussion of I/O is left for a later chapter it is worth
mentioning that BOOLEAN variables and constants can be printed
out using WRITE. If 'a' is a BOOLEAN variable then

WRITE(a)

will produce the word 'true' or 'false' on the screen according to the
value stored in 'a'. Notice that in standard Pascal you cannot READ
a BOOLEAN variable and in UCSD Pascal you cannot READ or
WRITE a BOOLEAN variable.

CHAR type

A variable of type CHAR can be used to store a single character. A
character in this context means any of the characters available in the
implementation of Pascal that you are using. This includes as a
minimum the alphabet A–Z, the digits 0–9 and the special characters , . * / = : ; ' (and). A variable of the type CHAR can be defined
by a **VAR** statement using the word CHAR. For example:

VAR ans,letter:CHAR;

defines the variables 'ans' and 'letter' to be of type CHAR. A constant of the type CHAR is simply a single character but, to make
sure that it isn't confused with a variable with a single letter name, a
CHAR constant must be enclosed in single quotes. For example:

'a' '9' '*' 'e' 'm'

74

are all constants of type CHAR and may be assigned to a variable of the same type. Some examples of CHAR assignment statements are:

    ans:='y';
    letter:='9'

If you want to use the constant that is simply the single quote itself then you must use '''' . As a general rule, if you want to represent the single quote you must write it twice.

There are no operators for combining variables of the type CHAR into expressions. This may make you think that there is very little that you can do with this data type, and to a certain extent this is true, but what you can do is very useful! Although there are no operators for the type CHAR there are four very important supplied functions—ORD, CHR, PRED and SUCC.

The functions ORD, CHR, PRED and SUCC

If you imagine all the characters that are available to be listed in some order then it is possible for you to go to that list and pick out any character given only its position in the list (e.g. the fifth character). The point is that the position in this ordered list is enough to define the character. The character set of any computer is in fact ordered but this order is not necessarily the same for all computers. You can usually assume that the letters are in alphabetical order and the digits are in numeric order but not that they will be all together in the list. That is, A will usually come before B but there may be characters in between them! Pascal provides two functions to allow access to the underlying order of the character set—ORD and CHR.

The function ORD(ch) returns the position (as an INTEGER) of the character 'ch' in the character set. As the data type of the parameter of ORD is CHAR and the data type of the result is INTEGER it can be thought of as forming a link between the two types; such functions are often called transfer functions.

The function CHR(i) is the opposite of the ORD function in that it returns the character that is in position i in the list. For example:

    CHR(25)

is the twenty-fifth character. The parameter of CHR is INTEGER and its result is CHAR so it too can be called a transfer function. The trouble with the CHR function is that different versions of Pascal number their character sets in different ways. Fortunately, most of the Pascals available on micros adopt the same convention and their character sets are numbered 0 to 255 but, for example, in OMSI Pascal, which is available on minicomputers, they are numbered from -128 to $+128$! If you use a number in CHR that does not correspond to a character you will get an error message, so take care how you use CHR if you want your programs to run on other machines. Notice that:

CHR(ORD(ch)) is ch

and

ORD(CHR(i)) is i

where 'ch' is any character and 'i' is any integer for which CHR is defined.

The main use for the ORD function is in allowing conditional expressions to be extended to include CHAR. Because ORD returns an INTEGER value, expressions like:

ORD('a')>3

or

ORD(ans)=ORD('y')

are perfectly valid. The expressions like

ORD(ans)=ORD('y')

are so important that Pascal allows them to be written as

ans='y'

thus giving the impression that CHAR types can be compared directly. This dropping of the ORD function extends to all the other relational operators; for example, you can write

ans>'y'

but you must never forget that this is just shorthand for

ORD(ans)>ORD('y')

In general, because of the lack of any fixed definition for the order of the character set, the only conditional expression that is entirely safe is equality.

The other two functions that can be used with data type CHAR are SUCC and PRED. Although they are of more use with other data types defined later in this chapter, CHAR type provides a simple introduction to their use and meaning. The function SUCC(ch) is the successor of the character 'ch'. The successor is simply the next character higher in the order, so a definition of SUCC is:

76

$$SUCC(ch)=CHR(ORD(ch)+1)$$

where 'ch' is any data of type CHAR. The function PRED(ch) is the predecessor of 'ch' and, as the predecessor is the character one lower in the order, a definition of PRED is:

$$PRED(ch)=CHR(ORD(ch)-1)$$

If we assume that the order of the character set is a to z then

SUCC('a') is b

and

PRED('b') is a

Notice that in this example PRED('a') and SUCC('z') are undefined. You can use the PRED and SUCC functions to move up and down through the character set—but beware of falling off the ends!

Reading and writing CHAR types

Unlike BOOLEAN type all versions of Pascal allow CHAR data to be both input using the READ statement and output using the WRITE statement. The statement:

WRITE(ch)

causes the single character stored in 'ch' to be printed out. The statement:

READ(ch)

causes the computer to wait until a single character has been typed on the keyboard to the variable 'ch'. For more information on character I/O see Chapter 8.

The use of CHAR data

There are so many uses of CHAR data that it is impossible to list them all. Characters are a fundamental method of communicating information to computers. A typical application would be to read in the answer to a question and use a conditional expression to decide what to do next. For example:

```
READ(ans);     (* read in a single character to ans *)
IF ans:='Y' THEN   action 1 ELSE action 2
rest of program
```

This sort of single-character answer can be extended to accepting complete words and we shall deal with this in Chapter 9 when we introduce strings. Apart from their use in answering questions, CHAR type are used to store written information in the computer and on backing store—tape and disk. Examples of these applications will be given in Chapters 8 and 9.

User-defined scalar types

The data types INTEGER, REAL, BOOLEAN and CHAR are all examples of scalar data types. The essential property of a scalar type is that the individual data items are ordered. We have already seen that the data type CHAR is put into order by the ORD function and INTEGER and REAL data types have an obvious order (e.g. $2<3$). It may be less obvious that for BOOLEAN type $true>false$ but we shall see that this is the case by the end of this section! To be precise, these data types are supplied scalar types. In Pascal it is possible for the user to define new scalar types by a method known as enumeration. Perhaps the best way to describe this is by an example.

Suppose that we want to define a variable that can be used to store which day of the week it is. We could use an INTEGER variable by coding the days of the week so that Monday corresponds to 1, Tuesday to 2 and so on to Sunday which corresponds to 7. Using this method any statements about the days of the week are written in terms of numbers. For example,

IF day=7 **THEN** . . . (* this checks to see if it is Sunday *)
day:=day+1   (* this moves on to the next day *)

The Pascal scalar type can be used to avoid this need to code the days of the week. It is possible to define a variable that can be used to store the days of the week by:

VAR day:(mon,tue,wed,thr,fri,sat,sun)

The list following the colon contains the only values that the variable 'day' can be used to store. Following this definition you can use 'day' in statements such as:

day:=mon

and, as we shall see later on, statements like

IF day=sun **THEN** . . .

Notice how much more directly connected with the idea of the days of the week these statements are compared with the INTEGER

78

coding method. The data type produced by this sort of definition is ordered and so it is an example of a Pascal scalar. The order is simply the order in which the items were written in the list. So in the above definition of days of the week the following is true:

mon<tue<wed<thur<fri<sat<sun

but it is important to notice that this ordering has nothing to do with the natural ordering of the days of the week; it is simply the order in which they were written. Another example might help to make this clear:

VAR colour:(blue,red,green,pink)

This definition of the variable 'colour' forces the following order on the four colours:

blue<red<green<pink

This should convince you that the ordering is produced only from the order that the names are written in the list and that this order may not make any good sense! The ordering of the data type BOOLEAN might now begin to make sense. In Pascal, defining a variable as of type BOOLEAN is the same as defining it as:

VAR state:(false,true)

which implies the ordering true>false!

There are no standard operators in Pascal for user-defined scalars but the three functions ORD, PRED and SUCC can be used with any scalar type except REAL. The three functions work in much the same way for all the scalars. The function ORD(scalar) returns the position in the order of 'scalar', PRED(scalar) returns the previous item in the order, and SUCC(scalar) returns the next item in the order. For user-defined scalar types the number of the order starts from zero. Just as in the case of CHAR if there is no next or previous element to 'scalar' then SUCC(scalar) and PRED(scalar) are undefined. Further consideration of the examples given above should help:

```
ORD(mon)      is 0
SUCC(mon)     is tue
PRED(red)     is blue
ORD(sun)      is 6
SUCC(pink)    is undefined
```

The SUCC and PRED functions are used to move up and down the ordering from one item to the next. The function ORD is used to extend conditional expressions to user-defined scalars. Again, as in the case of CHAR data, Pascal allows conditional expressions such as:

ORD(day)>ORD(mon)

to be written as

day>mon

Once again, it is important to remember that the results of such conditional expressions are governed by the values of the underlying ORD functions. The constants for a user-defined data type are the list of identifiers used in the definition of the type. It is important that the same identifier isn't used in more than one user-defined type. For example, it is wrong to use both:

VAR day:(mon,tue,wed,thur,fri,sat,sun)

and

VAR weekend:(sat,sun)

in the same program. The reason for this will be obvious if you try to work out the ordering when both definitions are present; according to the first **VAR** statement ORD(sat) is 5 but the second makes it 0. A constant can only have *one* position in an ordering.

Input and output of user-defined scalars

It is important to realise that Pascal does not provide any standard way of printing or reading user-defined scalar types. This may sound like a great difficulty but, as will be shown in Chapter 10, it is possible to construct procedures like READ and WRITE to print and read any user-defined scalar. The reason that Pascal doesn't provide such facilities as standard is that it is difficult to know how to print out or read in a general scalar type. INTEGER, REAL, CHAR and BOOLEAN present no problem because they have well-defined ways of being written down.

Using scalar types

Notice that the title of this section is 'Using scalar types' not 'Using user-defined scalar types'. The reason for this is that all scalar types can be used in the same way, irrespective of whether they are supplied or user-defined, with only two small exceptions. The scalar type REAL is better treated as a special case and user-defined data types cannot be printed or read using READ and WRITE (see last section). This means that:

1. Any scalar type except REAL can be used in ORD, PRED and SUCC.
2. All relational operators can be used to compare scalars.
3. Any scalar variable except REAL can be used as an index variable in a **FOR** statement.
4. Any scalar variable except REAL can be used to select one of a list of statements in a **CASE** statement.

Point 3 of this list means that you can write things like:

```
FOR day:=mon TO fri DO
                BEGIN worktime:=worktime+6;
                    IF  day<>wed  THEN  worktime:=
                    worktime+2
            END
```

which carries out the statement following the **DO** once for each day between 'mon' and 'fri'. The first time that the **DO** is carried out the index variable day takes on the value 'mon', the second 'tue' and so on to 'fri'. The **IF** statement tests the index variable to discover if the day is Wednesday, which is evidently early-closing day because an extra two hours is *not* added to 'worktime' in this case. The last point means that you can write things like:

```
CASE day OF
        mon,tue,thur,fri:workday:=true;
        wed:halfday:=true
        sat,sun:weekend:=true
            END
```

which will set one of the three variables 'workday', 'halfday' or 'weekday' to the value 'true' depending on the value of the variable 'day'.

In general, it is best to adopt the following rule: apart from printing and reading, anywhere you can use INTEGER you can substitute a user-defined scalar type.

User-defined data types

In the case of user-defined scalar types the definition involved listing each of the possible values that could be stored in the variable. This makes the **VAR** statement look complicated and different from its other forms. It would be an advantage to be able to use an identifier to stand in place of the list, and for it to be used in the same way as the type identifiers that we have already met, e.g. INTEGER, REAL, etc.

Pascal does allow the definition of new types (as we have seen in the last section) and new type identifiers by use of the **TYPE** statement. The general form of the **TYPE** statement is:

TYPE identifier = type

where 'identifier' is the name to be given to the newly created data type and 'type' is either the name of an existing data type or is a definition of a new type—i.e. a user-defined scalar. For example, in the last section the variable 'day' was defined to be one of the days of the week. This can now be done in two stages:

TYPE week=(mon,tue,wed,thur,fri,sat,sun);
VAR day:week;

The **TYPE** statement obviously has to be in the definition section of the program and has to come before any **VAR** statements. Once the new type has been defined then its identifier can be used in the same way as the names of the supplied types.

It is preferable to define a new type identifier and then use **VAR** statements to define the type of the variables that you are using because it usually makes the program easier to read and understand. Also, in the next chapter we will find other statements in which type identifiers can be used, where the use of type definitions would result in very long and difficult statements.

Subrange types

In the earlier section on user-defined scalar types it was explained that the two type definitions

VAR day:(mon,tue,wed,thur,fri,sat,sun);
VAR weekend:(sat,sun)

are not allowed in the same program because they cause difficulties with ORD(sat) and ORD(sun). However understandable this restriction is, it is annoying because the idea behind the two definitions is clear and reasonable. What we are trying to do is to create a variable, 'weekend', that can be used to store a subrange of the days of the week.

Pascal acknowledges this need by providing the ability to define a new data type that is a subrange of an existing type. The general form of a subrange definition is:

constant1 .. constant2

where ORD(constant1)<ORD(constant2). This defines a subrange of the data type to which both constants belong. The range of values that are valid for the new type is everything between and including constant1 and constant2. The definition can either be used in a **VAR** statement to define variables of the type or in a **TYPE** statement to give the new type a name. Some examples will help:

```
TYPE  weekday=(mon,tue,wed,thur,fri,sat,sun);
      workday=mon..fri;
      count=1..100;
      letter='a'..'z';
VAR   day:weekday;
      work:workday;
      index:count;
      ans1,ans2:letter
```

The **TYPE** statement defines four new data types. The first, 'weekday', is a user-defined scalar, the second is a subrange of 'weekday' consisting of the values 'mon', 'tue', 'wed', 'thur', 'fri'. The next two types, 'count' and 'letter', are included to show that subranges of supplied scalar types can be defined as subranges of INTEGER and CHAR respectively.

The **VAR** statement defines five variables of the newly defined types. The variable 'day' would be able to store values of 'weekday' from 'mon' to 'sun' but 'work' is only able to store values from 'mon' to 'fri'. Notice that the values of the functions ORD, PRED and SUCC are defined by their values on the complete data type— 'work' is a subrange of 'weekday'. The variable 'index' can only store values of type INTEGER between (and including) 1 and 100, and 'ans1' and 'ans2' can only be used to store letters.

You are free to define subrange types of any scalar type with one exception: you cannot define a subrange of the type REAL.

The importance of subrange types should be obvious; if you only want to use a subrange of a data type then it is good practice to state the range that you expect to use. If for some reason the value of a variable goes outside this range then presumably there is an error in your program. If you have defined the variable to be a subrange type then this will be detected while the program is running and an error message will be printed. For example, if you know that the variable should always be a positive INTEGER then defining the type:

TYPE posint=0..MAXINT

will make sure that any variables that are of type 'posint' are positive. Another reason for using subranges wherever possible is that some versions of Pascal will try to use the smallest amount of computer memory to store a data type and a subrange can often be squeezed into a smaller space than the original type.

The rules for working with a subrange type are the same as its original type. For example:

    index:=index+3
    work:=SUCC(mon)

You can use a subrange type as if it were the same as its original type as long as the value that you try to store in it is within its range of definition. This means that the following is valid:

VAR a:INTEGER;b:0..30
BEGIN
            a:=10;
            b:=a+2

It also means that if you can use WRITE and READ to print and input a data type you can also use them with subranges of the type. In short, anywhere you can use a particular type you can use a subrange of that type and vice versa—as long as the data stored in any subrange type is within the defined subrange.

Summary

In this chapter we have introduced the final two standard data types, BOOLEAN and CHAR. Two ways of constructing new data types have also been described: user-defined scalars and subrange types. The **TYPE** statement was also described as a way of giving names to the new types.

Questions

1. If a:=3;b:=4 work out the following BOOLEAN expressions:
    —(a>b)**OR**(b=4)
    —(a=b)**AND**(a>5)
    —**NOT**(a=b)
    —(a<4)**AND**(b=4)**OR**(a=b)

2. Write a **VAR** statement defining variables suitable for storing the following:
    —the answer to a question;
    —the result of (a=b);

—the months of the year;
—the hour of the day in a 24-hour clock;
—the hour of the day in a 12-hour clock.

3. Write a **TYPE** statement to name the types of those variables in question 2 that are user-defined types.

4. Write a **FOR** statement that will print out all the characters from 'a' to 'z' without using the CHR function.

8
Input/output—sequential files

It may come as a surprise that the subject of input/output (I/O) has been left to so late a chapter; after all, any program is useless unless it can communicate with the outside world. The reason for putting off consideration of I/O to this late stage is that Pascal I/O is very logical and easy to understand if explained from a slightly more advanced point of view than that of a complete beginner. It is not until the idea of procedure and data types in general have been appreciated that the subject of I/O can be treated in full. Until this stage is reached the use of the READ and WRITE statements to input and print single variables is sufficient to be able to write useful if not particularly well finished programs.

It is important to realise that the rather limited use of I/O in the example programs up to this point in the book is not to be taken as a suggestion that the way a program gets its data from, or gives results to, the outside world is unimportant. A good program is one that reads data in a simple, efficient way and prints results that are self-explanatory and clear.

Communicating with the outside world is only one part of I/O in Pascal. Most computers have some form of backing store—for example, a tape or disk drive—and the reading and writing of information to and from such devices is also part of I/O. In theory, Pascal treats all I/O in the same way. It should be possible to read and write data without worrying where it is to come from or where it is to go to. In practice, experience is very different. Different versions of Pascal treat backing store in different ways and it is often necessary to distinguish between I/O from and to an interactive device, such as a terminal or the integral screen and keyboard of a microcomputer, and other automatic devices such as disks and tapes.

I/O is an area of Pascal where there are major divergences from one single standard. This presents a problem of how to present the topic. If it is presented as a series of special cases then the underlying logic and simplicity are hidden. On the other hand if only the logic is described then I/O will seem an easy subject but the knowledge will be of no practical value! The solution adopted here is to discuss, in this chapter, the overall principles and working of standard Pascal's I/O and describe briefly the variations needed to use the various popular implementations of Pascal in Appendix 4.

The only real difficulty with this approach is that any examples given in the text, although illustrating the point accurately, may not work on *your* system because of some very small (and unimportant) difference between your system and standard Pascal. This does not mean that you should not try the programs as you go along; indeed they should be used to discover the consequences, if any, of the differences in your implementation.

The sequential file—an advanced data type

A sequential file can be thought of as a list of data items, each item of the same type. Unlike the sequences or lists that we are most familiar with, however, there is a restriction on how we are allowed to read or alter a sequential file. You can only gain access to the data items one at a time. This is rather like looking through a window to read the data items. Only one item can be seen at a time but you can move the window up and down the list to read other items.

Pascal files are even more restrictive than this. To understand how they work, think of a file as a long strip of paper that data can be read from or written to, but only through a small movable window (see *Fig.* 8.1). Although the window is small it must be big enough to allow a single data item to be read or written without moving the window! When reading an existing file you must start with the window at the beginning and, each time you read an item, the window moves one item towards the end of the file. If you want to re-read the file then you can reposition the window at the start and go through it again, but you cannot move the window backwards to re-read an item.

Writing, or creating, sequential files is also subject to similar restrictions. A brand-new file has no data elements in it—it is said to be empty. Data items can be added to it one at a time to increase its length, in theory without limit but in practice only to a very large maximum that depends on the system that you are using. Each data item is written to the file through the window; after it has been written the window moves one place along to an empty space (see Fig. 8.2).

When reading a sequential file it would be an obvious advantage if there were some way of detecting that the last item had been read. The easiest way to achieve this is by writing a special mark, an end

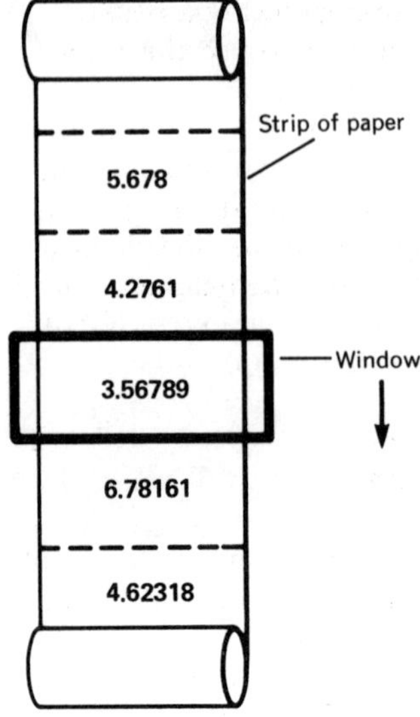

Fig. 8.1. Reading a sequential file

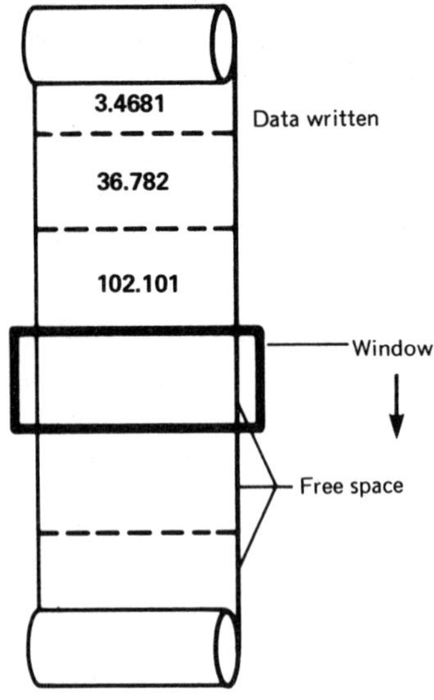

Fig. 8.2. Creating a sequential file

of file mark, following the last item on the file. Reading this mark is a signal that all the data items have been read.

Sequential files in Pascal

Sequential files are available in Pascal as yet another data type, **FILE**, although in this case the data type is different from any we have met so far; it is itself an organisation of other data types. Data types that are the result of imposing an organisation on other data types are very important in Pascal and are known as structured types. They are dealt with in detail in Chapter 9.

A variable can be defined to be of type **FILE** using a **VAR** statement like

VAR data :**FILE OF** INTEGER

Notice that it is of the same form as all the other **VAR** statements that we have examined. It defines the variable data to be a sequential file of INTEGERs. There are two parts to the type definition: the word **FILE** makes 'data' a sequential file but you also need to say what type of item can be stored as part of the sequence—this is where the **OF** INTEGER part comes in. The general definition of a **FILE** is:

VAR list of variable names:**FILE OF** data type

You can replace 'data type' with any valid Pascal type but it is rare to find **FILE OF FILE** actually implemented! The **TYPE** statement can also be used to introduce new type identifiers for files. For example:

TYPE TEXT=**FILE OF** CHAR;
VAR chap1,chap2,chap3:TEXT

first defines a new type TEXT to be a file of characters and then defines 'chap1', 'chap2' and 'chap3' to be of this type, i.e. files of characters. The type **FILE OF** CHAR is so important that it is given the special name TEXT automatically by Pascal.

File handling

Although **FILE** is a standard data type it should be obvious, from the ways that a sequential file can be read and written, that something other than an assignment statement is needed to handle the type. A **FILE** is defined by a **VAR** statement as if it were an ordinary variable, but it is very different because it can store more than a single value. However, associated with every **FILE** is a simple variable of the same underlying type as the data stored in the file. This variable is referred to as a buffer variable and, if the name of the file is 'F', then the name of the buffer variable is 'F^'. For example, the file data defined as a **FILE OF** INTEGER in the previous section has an associated buffer variable 'data^', which is also of type INTEGER.

The procedure for adding an item to a file has two steps. First the item must be assigned to the buffer variable and then the standard procedure PUT must be used to carry out the operation of writing the contents of the buffer variable to the file. For example, to write an INTEGER to the file 'data' the pair of instructions,

```
data^:=1;
PUT(data)
```

should be used. Notice that the PUT is given the name of the file rather than the name of the buffer variable.

Things are not quite as simple as this because we have to worry about where the data item will be written in the sequence of data in the file. Before the first item is written out to the file the supplied procedure REWRITE(filename) must be used to make sure that the file is empty and that the window is at the start. After this the file behaves as a normal sequential file. The operation of clearing the file and getting it ready for the first write operation is known as opening the file for writing.

Before data items can be read from a file the file must be prepared. In particular the window must be moved back to the start of the file. This is known as opening the file for reading and is carried out by the supplied procedure RESET(filename). The procedure RESET not only moves the window back to the start of the file but also places the first item into the file's buffer variable. As the buffer variable can be used as an ordinary Pascal variable this means that the first item of the file is available to be used in expressions, assignment statements, etc, immediately after the RESET. The next and subsequent items of the file can be read into the buffer variable using the supplied procedure GET(filename).

For example, if the file data used in the last example is supposed to contain a list of ten INTEGER values then the following program fragment would read the values and add them up:

```
total:=0; (* set zero total of an INTEGER variable to 0 *)
RESET(data); (* positions window at start
                        and GETs first item into data^ *)
```

FOR i:=1 **TO** 10 **DO**   (* i is an INTEGER *)
      BEGIN total:=total+data^; (* add item to total *)
          GET(data)   (* get next item into data^ *)
    END

This example only works if there are at least 10 INTEGERs in the file data. If there are fewer, then the program tries to read beyond the end of the file! This is where the Pascal function EOF comes into its own. The last item in any file is the special symbol marking the end of the file. The EOF function is a BOOLEAN function that is true if the file's window is over the end of file mark and false otherwise.

We now know enough to be able to rewrite the last example so that it will add together *all* the items on the file data without knowing in advance how many there are:

total:=0;   (* zero total an INTEGER variable *)
RESET(data); (* open data for reading *)
WHILE EOF(data)=false **DO**
      BEGIN total:=total+data^;
          GET(data)
    END

The **WHILE** loop continues until the EOF function returns the value true. This happens when the GET function finally moves the window past the last useful data item and positions it over the end of file mark. Notice that when this happens the value of the buffer variable is undefined and should not be used. If you try to use GET to move the window beyond the end of file mark the program will stop and an error message will be printed.

The instructions:

filename^:=variable;PUT(filename)

and

variable:=filename^;GET(filename)

occur so often that most versions of Pascal provide the standard procedures

WRITE(filename, variable)

and

READ(filename, variable)

that can be used in their place. Once again, the previous example can be rewritten:

```
total:=0;
RESET(data);
WHILE EOF(data)=false DO
        BEGIN READ(data,i);
              total:=total+i
        END
```

Notice that the use of READ means that we have to introduce an extra INTEGER variable 'i'. It is important to notice that READ and WRITE are only defined for TEXT files in standard Pascal but most Pascal implementations allow their use with any type of file.

Summary of reading and writing files

It would be useful to gather together all that we have learned about the Pascal data type **FILE** and its associated functions.

Files in general

A FILE is a sequence of data items all of the same type. A file can be defined using a **VAR** or a **TYPE** statement and the specification **FILE OF** type—where type can be any other Pascal type. If the name of the file is 'F' then there is an associated buffer variable 'F^' of the same type as the data items in the file.

Writing files

REWRITE(F)—the file 'F' is emptied of any existing data and made ready for writing. The state of EOF is set to true.
PUT(F)—writes the contents of 'F^' to the current position in the file and moves the current position on one. The value of EOF(file) *must* be true before using PUT(F).
EOF(F)—is (and must be) true while a file is being written.
WRITE(F,variable)—assigns the contents of variable to 'F^' and then does a PUT(F).

Reading files

RESET(F)—moves the window to the start of the file, and assigns the first item to 'F^'.

92

GET(F)—moves the window over the next item and loads it into 'F^'. EOF must be true before GET is used.

READ(F,variable)—is the same as variable:=F^;GET(F).

Notice that the condition that EOF must be true before PUT is used means that you cannot write to a file while you are reading it: before you can write to a file you must use REWRITE and this erases any old data that you may have been reading. Similarly you cannot read a file while you are writing it because REWRITE sets EOF to true and GET will only work if EOF is false. This exclusion means that you cannot selectively change a file, you must either read it or write it.

Text files–formatting

As was mentioned earlier the type **FILE OF** CHAR is so important that Pascal provides the identifier TEXT defined to be the same type. That is:

VAR chap1:**FILE OF** CHAR

and

VAR chap1:TEXT

mean the same thing.

There are two standard text files available on every Pascal implementation: INPUT and OUTPUT. These correspond to the normal system input and output devices, e.g. a keyboard and a screen, and must not be defined using a **VAR** statement. As most I/O deals with these two devices, if the file specification is left out of any file commands except GET and PUT the files INPUT and OUTPUT are used, i.e. INPUT is the default input file and OUTPUT is the default output file. For example, READ(ans) is the same as READ(INPUT,ans). We will return to the files INPUT and OUTPUT in the next section.

The reason why text files are so important is that text files form the only way that a computer can communicate with humans. You may think that you could look at a **FILE OF** INTEGER and read off the various numbers stored there. This is not the case because the numbers in a **FILE OF** INTEGER would be written in an internal format that is suitable only for the computer to read. When a human thinks of an INTEGER it is usually a string of digits that is brought to mind but a computer stores an INTEGER in binary, as a string of zeros and ones. It should be realised that a digit that can be read or written is in fact a constant of type CHAR!

In the previous chapters we have used the procedure WRITE(variable) to print out the contents of 'variable'. Although it has been passed off without very much comment, WRITE carries out quite a complex task if 'variable' is not of type CHAR. For in this case it takes the contents of 'variable' and transforms it into a string of characters and/or digits and then it prints out these characters for us to look at. It is sometimes difficult to understand that this transformation is necessary for INTEGERs and REALs as we are so used to writing them down as strings of characters. It is slightly more obvious in the case of BOOLEAN type. The representation of 'true' and 'false' inside the computer is not in terms of the words true and false. The internal representation is more compact than a string of letters and amounts to storing a binary 1 for true and a binary 0 for false. Now if 'ans' is a variable of type BOOLEAN consider the statement WRITE(ans). The contents of 'ans' will be either 0 or 1 but what is printed out is either the character string 'false' or the character string 'true' because they are better understood by humans. In short, binary codes are for computers and characters are for humans.

The procedures READ and WRITE can now be seen in a fuller light. When used on text files they allow data types other than CHAR to be read and written directly to the file. They are no longer simply equivalent to

GET(F);variable:=F^

and

F^:=variable;PUT(F)

Instead, READ reads in a string of characters and converts it to the correct data type, WRITE converts the data type to a string of characters and writes each one on to the file.

Because of the use of text files to communicate with humans there are a number of extra features that have been provided to aid in this role. The first is the provision of an additional special symbol similar to the end of file mark, which is used to divide the file up into lines of characters. This special symbol is known as an end of line mark and it has an accompanying BOOLEAN function EOLN(filename) which is false if the character under the window is not the end of line symbol and true if it is. The end of line symbol is never read into the buffer variable because it is not of type CHAR; instead the buffer variable is loaded with a blank. End of line symbols can be written into a text file by the use of the supplied procedure WRITELN(variable), but as the procedures READ and WRITE operate differently on text files a consideration of WRITELN is left until a little later.

Reading and writing a text file is limited to the data type CHAR if the functions GET and PUT are used. To allow the reading and writing of other data types to a text file the supplied procedures READ(F,chr) and WRITE(F,chr) have been heavily modified and, as mentioned previously, are no longer simply equivalent to

variable:=F^;GET(F)

and

F^;=variable;PUT(F)

respectively. Not only will WRITE, when working with text files, accept variables that are not of type CHAR, but also extra parameters that determine the way that these variables will be printed out. The trouble is that the way these extra parameters control the format of the printout depends on the type of variable used in the WRITE statement. We will deal with the operation of WRITE for each of the three data types with which it can be used in turn.

INTEGER

The general form of an INTEGER WRITE is:

WRITE(variable:m)

where 'm' is a number indicating the number of characters that are to be used to print the constants of the variable. If ':m' is omitted then an implementation-dependent default value will be used. For example,

WRITE(count:4)

means:write the contents of the variable 'count' using four characters. If the number in 'count' can be written in less than four characters then blanks will be printed in front of the number to make the number of characters used equal to four. However, if the number is bigger than four digits the specification will be ignored and the number will be printed using as many characters as necessary.

REAL

The general form of a REAL WRITE is:

WRITE(variable:m:n)

where 'm' is a number indicating the total number of characters that are to be used to print the contents of the variable, and 'n' is a number that specifies the number of digits that should follow the decimal point. For example:

WRITE(area:5:2)

means that the contents of the variable 'area' will be written using a total of five characters, two of which will follow the decimal point. If the number can be written in fewer than five characters then blanks will be printed in front of the number to make up the number of characters to five. If the number takes more than five characters no blanks are printed and the number is printed in full. If the fractional part does not fit into two characters then it is rounded. If 'area' contains 4.54342, WRITE (area:5:2) will print one blank and 4.54. (Notice that the decimal point is counted as one character!) Both 'm' and 'n' may be omitted. If 'n' is omitted then the number will be printed using 'm' characters in exponential form (see Chapter 3.) If 'm' is also omitted an implementation-dependent default value will be substituted for 'm'.

CHAR and strings

The general form of a CHAR WRITE is fairly uninteresting. The statement:

WRITE(variable)

simply writes one character with no special formatting. However, Pascal recognises the need for printing questions and other messages on the screen and so allows a string of characters to be used as a parameter of WRITE. A string of characters is simply a number of characters surrounded by single quotes; e.g. 'this is a string'. Notice that the string is between the quotes; i.e. the string does not include the quotes, they simply show where it starts and stops. The general form of the WRITE for a string is;

WRITE('string':m)

which causes the string to be printed out using a total of 'm' characters. If the string is shorter than 'm', blanks are printed to fill the space. If the string is longer than 'm' then only the first 'm' characters are printed. For example:

WRITE('hello':8)

will print three blanks and then the word 'hello'. If 'm' is omitted the string is printed as written without any extra blanks or loss of characters; that is, the default value of 'm' is the length of the string.

BOOLEAN

The general form is:

WRITE(variable:m)

The BOOLEAN variable causes the word true or false to be printed. From the point of view of formatting, BOOLEAN variables are treated in the same way as strings; that is, enough blanks are printed to use 'm' characters. For example, if 'ans' is true then:

WRITE(ans:10)

prints six blanks and then the word true. (Note that not all versions of Pascal allow BOOLEAN to be used in WRITE; in particular, UCSD does not.)

The general form of WRITE

Although the details given above may seem a little confusing they all fall into a general pattern:

WRITE(e:m)

where 'e' is a variable and 'm' is a number (often called the field width). The number 'm' indicates how many characters are to be used to print the contents of the variable 'e'. If the contents can be printed using fewer characters than the field width then enough blanks are printed first to make up the number to 'm'. This is known as printing the data right justified in a field width 'm'. This can be thought of as assigning an amount of space 'm' to the printing of the data item and moving it over to the far right of the space—hence the term right justified. For example:

WRITE('Total To Date':20)

can be thought of as printing the string hard over to the right of a 20-character field. In practice this means that the string starts in the eighth place:

```
          11111111112
 12345678901234567890
       Total  To  Date
```

This right justification works for all valid data types. The only real difference is the way that the data is printed when the field width is too small. In the case of character and string data the answer is that as much of the string as possible is printed in the field allowed. For example:

    WRITE('Total To Date':7)

produces

    1234567
    Total T

While this might be a suitable solution for strings, this chopping-off to fit the field width would cause havoc if applied to numeric data. Imagine the problems of using a program that would print 100 when the answer was 100000 just because the field width was specified as 3! The only sensible solution for numeric data is to ignore the field width and use as much space as needed, which is what actually happens.

The only exception to these general rules applies to REAL data. When printing REAL data it is obvious that apart from controlling the number of characters used it is necessary to control the number of digits following the decimal point. For example, if the area of a circle has been calculated from a rough measurement in metres it makes no sense to print the answer as something like 5.24583058. Thus a second parameter is allowed, in this case indicating the number of digits after the decimal point. The extra digits are removed by rounding the number.

There is one other extension to WRITE, which in this case also applies to READ. You can use as many parameters in a READ or a WRITE as necessary. This simple extension allows statements such as:

    WRITE('The area of the circle is ',area:8:2)

which is equivalent to

    WRITE('The area of the circle is ');
    WRITE(area:8:2)

Similarly,

    READ(radius1,radius2,radius3)

is equivalent to:

    READ(radius1);READ(radius2);READ(radius3);

The only area of formatting that we have not covered in detail so far is how to start a new line. As mentioned earlier, text files have another special symbol associated with them—the end of line character. This can be written into text files to divide them up into a set of lines. These lines correspond to the usual idea of a line of text displayed on a computer screen or printed on a printer. The end of line marker also corresponds to the key marked RETURN or ENTER on most computer key-boards; that is, pressing RETURN or ENTER sends an end of line character. To place a data value on a new line it is necessary to separate it from previous values by an end of line symbol. The procedure WRITELN (briefly introduced in Chapter 2) will write such an end of line symbol and can be used in two ways:

1. Using WRITELN in place of WRITE writes an end of line symbol after all the variables have been printed out.
2. WRITELN can be used without any parameters to write an end of line symbol.

Therefore,

WRITE(ans1,ans2);WRITELN

is equivalent to

WRITELN(ans1,ans2)

To see how WRITE and WRITELN differ consider the output produced by the following short examples:

```
WRITE('the first root    =',root1:8:5);
WRITE('the second root   =',root2:8:5)
```

and

```
WRITELN('the first root    =',root1:8:5);
WRITELN('the second root =',root2:8:5)
```

The first example will print everything on the same line whereas the second will print each answer on a different line. The second WRITELN is in fact not necessary to produce each answer on a different line but it does ensure that the next WRITE will start on a fresh line and not be added on to the second answer.

There is a READ equivalent of WRITELN called READLN. The easiest way to describe how READLN works is by a short line of Pascal. READLN is equivalent to:

BEGIN WHILE NOT EOLN(F) **DO** GET(F);GET(F) **END**

You should be able to work out what this means. A READLN will move the window through the file 'F' and leave it positioned over the first character following the next end of line symbol. That is, READLN skips to the start of the next line. You can also use READLN in the same way as READ and in this case the variables are read in and then the window is moved to the start of the next line. So

    READLN(data1,data2,data3)

is the same as

    READ(data1,data2,data3);READLN

It is important to notice that although most of the examples in this section have been in terms of READ and WRITE using the default text file INPUT and OUTPUT, everything discussed applies to any text file. The only change required is to introduce the appropriate file name into the file handling statements. For example, READ (variable) becomes READ(filename,variable) and EOLN becomes EOLN(filename), etc.

Standard text files—INPUT and OUTPUT

Although we have already mentioned the standard text files INPUT and OUTPUT in the last section there are a number of special features that still need to be considered.

While it is obvious that the file INPUT cannot be used for writing and OUTPUT cannot be used for reading, it is less obvious that RESET and REWRITE cannot be used on either file. The reason for this restriction is that no obvious interpretation can be given to RESET(INPUT) and REWRITE(OUTPUT) because of the physical properties of the input and output devices normally associated with INPUT and OUTPUT. However, they are implicitly carried out at the start of every program before any I/O has been carried out and this brings problems of its own.

The standard version of Pascal expects the INPUT file to be associated with a card reader and OUTPUT to be associated with a shared line-printer. In this case any data that the program needs to read in must be punched on cards and available before the program is run. These days most computers allow an interactive way of inputting data using a keyboard and a display screen. This causes a number of problems for standard Pascal.

The standard procedure RESET automatically reads in the first character in the text file into the associated buffer variable. This works when a deck of cards is the INPUT file: it simply means that the first character on the first card is read in. But if a keyboard is the

100

INPUT file then it cannot be opened (and the program cannot continue) until a character has been typed. The solution to this problem differs according to which implementation of Pascal you are using. Most simply load the buffer variable with a harmless character such as a blank, but UCSD Pascal uses a new file type—interactive. Interactive files are text files but the initial RESET does not load the buffer variable with the first character in the file. This means that the normal definition of READ(F,chr) as chr:=F^;GET(F) must be changed to GET(F);chr:=F^.

If all this sounds excessively complicated don't worry too much because in practice any implementation of Pascal is arranged to work with INPUT and OUTPUT much as you would expect it to—unless you want to use GET and PUT in some clever way!

External files

So far we have treated files as if they were created by the program, existed for as long as the program was running and were then destroyed. Files used in this way are called local files. The more usual case is that the files are created on some storage device such as a disk or tape and exist after the program is finished. Such files are known as external files. Thus it is possible for a program to find that a file it opens for reading via a RESET(F) already has data in it.

The only extra complication in using external files is that the name by which the Pascal program knows a file need not be the same as the name that the rest of the computer system uses. The name that the rest of the system uses is known as the external name of the file and is the name that would appear on any catalogue of the device that the file is stored on. There are two basic ways of making the connection between Pascal filenames and external filenames. Such implementations introduce new statements and others modify existing statements. A very common method (e.g. UCSD) is to add an extra parameter to the RESET and REWRITE procedures; for example,

    RESET(F,external filename)
    REWRITE(F, external filename)

where 'F' is the Pascal filename. Even for versions of Pascal that use the same method, there are often incompatibilities in external filenames; for example, one may allow eight-letter names and another nine.

Standard Pascal does not allow any difference between the internal and external filename. An external file is created by using its name as a parameter in the PROGRAM statement in the same way as INPUT and OUTPUT appear. This is the way that all our subsequent examples will handle external files; it is up to you to change them to fit your implementation.

The details of how individual implementations handle external file names and details of other specific file handling facilities can be found in Appendix 4.

Some examples of I/O

1. A program to print out any multiplication table in the 'standard form':

```
PROGRAM table(INPUT,OUTPUT);
VAR i,n,ans:INTEGER;
BEGIN
        WRITELN;
        WRITE('which table—e.g. type 2 for two times table ');
        READ(n);
        WRITELN;WRITELN;
        FOR i:=1 TO 12 DO
                BEGIN
                        ans:=i*n;
                        WRITELN(i:3,'*',n:3,'=',ans:3)
                END;
        WRITELN
END.
```

Notice the use of WRITELN to produce new lines, the use of WRITE followed by READ to ask a question and receive an answer and the use of field widths to make the table line up in columns.

2. A program to copy a non-text external file (in this example the type of the file is REAL):

```
PROGRAM copy(INPUT,OUTPUT,infile,outfile);
VAR infile,outfile FILE OF REAL;
BEGIN
        RESET(infile);REWRITE(outfile);
        WHILE NOT EOF(infile) DO
                BEGIN outfile^:=infile^;
                        PUT(outfile);
                        GET(infile)
                END
END.
```

(Remember that because this program uses external files it might not work on your system without some small changes—see Appendix 4.) Notice that the first assignment of buffer variables occurs before the first PUT and GET because RESET loads the first item into 'infile^'.

3. A program to create a text file from the keyboard:

```
PROGRAM edit(INPUT,OUTPUT,note);
VAR note:text;
     ch:CHAR;
BEGIN
     REWRITE(note);
     WHILE NOT EOF(INPUT) DO
       BEGIN
          READ(ch);
          IF NOT EOLN(INPUT) THEN
                              WRITE(note,ch)
                              ELSE
                              WRITELN(note)
       END
END.
```

Notice the way the EOLN function is used to select between writing 'ch' or an end of line mark. To stop this program you need to find out what key or keys send an end of file symbol. For example, in Pascal/M pressing CONTROL and z sends an end of file symbol.

Summary

In this chapter the idea of a **FILE** type was introduced. The basic methods of handling files using PUT and GET were explained along with the function EOF. Text files were introduced as a basic means of communication and the procedures READ and WRITE were explained. The line structure of a text file was examined and the function EOL and the procedures READLN and WRITELN were explained. Finally the idea of interactive and external files was discussed.

Questions

1. Write file definitions for:
   —a file of INTEGERs;

—a file to be displayed on an output device;
—a file of days of the week.

2. Write a program that will read a file created using program 'edit' given in Example 3 and display it on the screen.

3. Go back to earlier examples and change any REAL values printed out in exponent form to the more normal 'decimal point' form.

9
Structured types

In the last chapter we examined the data type **FILE** and commented on the fact that it is different from other Pascal data types in that it is made up from other data types. This idea of organising more funda-mental data types can be generalised to give a wide and varied range of new data types—structured types. The process of organising is known as a structuring method. Pascal provides four structuring methods: the **FILE** that we have already met, the **ARRAY**, the **RECORD** and the **SET**. We will deal with each of these new types in turn.

The ARRAY

The idea of an array is best introduced by an example. Consider the problem of reading in five characters and writing them out in reverse order. Although we can solve this problem using the knowledge of Pascal that we already have, the solution is not very inspiring:

```
PROGRAM rev(INPUT,OUTPUT);
VAR c1,c2,c3,c4,c5:CHAR;
BEGIN
        READ(c1,c2,c3,c4,c5);
        WRITE(c5,c4,c3,c2,c1)
END
```

Changing this program to reverse, say, twenty characters would start to show up problems! If you look at the program however it gives a clue as to what is needed to solve the problem. If we could write 'ci', where 'i' was an INTEGER variable, to pick out one of the set of variables 'c1' to 'c5' then we could use a **FOR** statement to read in the characters—something along the lines of:

FOR i:=1 **TO** 5 **DO** READ(ci)

You can think of 'ci' as one of a row of five integer variables. The name of the row is 'c' and any particular variable can be picked out by writing its number alongside the name.

In Pascal this collection of variables under a common name is called an **ARRAY**. The variable or constant used to select a particular variable from the collection is called the index. To avoid confusion with other variables (the variable 'ci' for example) the single variable picked out by the index 'i' is written as 'c[i]' and is known as an element of the array. The definition of the **ARRAY** 'c' of five variables of type CHAR is via a **VAR** statement:

VAR c:**ARRAY** [1..5] **OF** CHAR

The part of the statement following the colon, as always, defines the type of the variable. The 1..5 between the square brackets indicates the size of the **ARRAY** and that the first element is 'c[1]' and the last is 'c[5]'. Following the **OF** is the type identifier CHAR indicating that each element is of this type. We can now rewrite the previous program using an array:

```
PROGRAM rev(INPUT,OUTPUT);
VAR c:ARRAY [1..5] OF CHAR;
    i:INTEGER;
BEGIN
      FOR i:=1 TO 5 DO READ(c[i]);
      FOR i:=5 DOWNTO 1 DO WRITE(c[i]);
END.
```

The only extra point to notice in this example is the use of the **DOWNTO** to print 'c' in reverse order.

In general, the **ARRAY** in Pascal can have any data type for its elements. The type of the index variable is also not limited to INTEGER. If you look back at the **VAR** statement defining 'c', the specification for the upper and lower limits for the index, i.e. [1..5], you should recognise a subrange type. In general, the index variable can be any subrange type or a scalar except for INTEGER and REAL. The number of elements that the **ARRAY** has is simply the number of different values that the subrange or scalar type can take on. The general definition of an **ARRAY** can now be written as:

VAR variable:**ARRAY** [type1] **OF** type2;

where 'type1' is any subrange type or scalar type except INTEGER or REAL, and 'type2' is any type (with the exception of **FILE**). Some examples of valid **ARRAY** definitions are:

```
TYPE day=(mon,tue,wed,thur,fri,sat,sun);
     month=1..12;
VAR a:ARRAY [5..10] OF REAL;
    b:ARRAY [day] OF BOOLEAN;
    c:ARRAY [month] OF INTEGER;
```

The first **ARRAY** 'a' is a collection of REAL elements, the first of which is 'a[5]' and the last 'a[10]'. The **ARRAY** 'b' is a collection of seven BOOLEAN variables, the first of which is 'b[mon]' and the last 'b[sun]'. The **ARRAY** 'c' is a collection of 12 INTEGER variables, the first of which is 'c[1]' and the last 'c[12]'. To help make clear the idea of using a scalar type to define an **ARRAY**, the **ARRAY** 'b' can be imagined as:

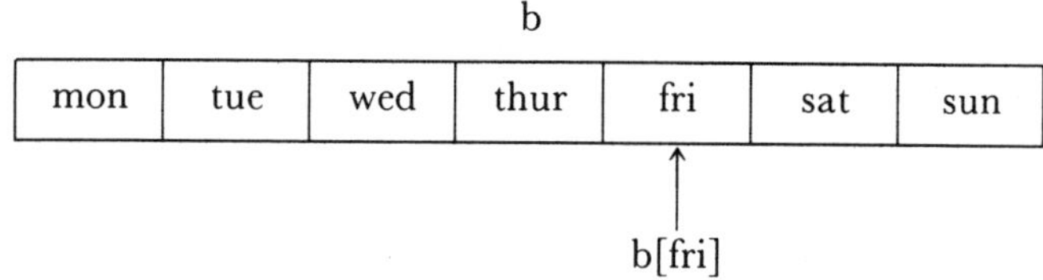

Some valid assignments to these **ARRAY**s are:

    a[6]:=5.5;
    b[tue]:=true;
    c[4]:=30

The index can be a variable as well as a constant and is only subject to the restriction that the type of the index variable must either be of the same type or of the type from which the subrange is derived. It is also possible to use an expression as an index and, once again, the only restriction is that it must evaluate to the same type or to the type from which the subrange is derived.

As it is possible to write

    month[i]:=30

with 'i' an INTEGER not in the subrange 1..12, you could specify by accident an element that doesn't exist. For example:

    i:=13;
    month[i]

This will cause the program to stop and an error message to be printed.

Some more examples of valid assignments using the above arrays, this time using expressions, are:

    a[i+1]:=a[i]+a[i+1]; (* valid if i+1 is in the range 5..10 *)
    b[succ(mon)]:=b[mon]; (* always valid *)
    c[2*i]:=30; (* valid if 2*i is in the range 1..12 *)

Notice that array elements can be used anywhere that a simple variable of the same type can. Although the range of operations for array elements isn't limited, the same isn't true of entire arrays. As an

107

array has a single name you might think that it can be used as a single entity but the only operation that an entire array can be involved in is assignment. For example, if 'data1' and 'data2' are two arrays then assignment of every element of 'data1' to 'data2' can be written:

    data1:=data2

This can only be done if the two arrays are of identical type, i.e. the same number and type of elements and the same type of index. So the following definition of 'data1' and 'data2' would allow direct assignment:

VAR data1,data2:**ARRAY** [1..10] **OF** REAL

but

VAR data1:**ARRAY** [1..10] **OF** REAL;data2:**ARRAY** [0..9] **OF** REAL

would not, because although in the second case the number and type of the elements in 'data1' and 'data2' are the same the index types are different! To assign 'data1' to 'data2' with the second definition you would have to use:

FOR i:=0 **TO** 9 **DO** data2[i]:=data1[i+1];

Strings and packing

The way Pascal stores arrays is in general of no interest to the programmer. The one exception is that Pascal allows the use of the word **PACKED** to indicate that the array should be stored in as little space as possible. Saving memory space seems like such a good idea that it might be tempting always to specify **PACKED** in every array definition. The trouble is that the way an array is stored affects the time it takes to locate a particular element and it is almost a law of computing that economising on memory makes things take longer! So there is a trade-off between using standard arrays that are fast but take more memory and **PACKED ARRAY**s that are slow but save memory.

The general definition of a **PACKED ARRAY** is:

VAR variable:**PACKED ARRAY** type1 **OF** type2;

The only change from the previous **ARRAY** definition is the use of the word **PACKED**. It is important to realise that a **PACKED ARRAY** can be used exactly the same way as an ordinary **ARRAY** but it is of a different type. For example:

108

VAR a:**PACKED ARRAY** [1..10] **OF** CHAR;
      b:**ARRAY** [1..10] **OF** CHAR;

The variable 'a' is an array of characters: the first element is 'a[1]' and the last is 'a[10]'. The variable 'b' is also an array of characters; the first element is 'b[1]' and the last is 'b[10]', but it is not the same type as 'a', i.e. the statement 'a:=b' is not allowed.

Because of the extra time sometimes required to process a **PACKED ARRAY**, it is useful to be able to convert part (or even all) of it to an unpacked form. This can be done simply by assigning each element to be converted to an element of an ordinary array. For example, to unpack the array 'a' into 'b' defined in the previous example we could use:

FOR i:=1 **TO** 10 **DO** b[i]:=a[i];

To unpack an entire array into a larger one, Pascal provides the procedure UNPACK(array1,array2,start) which will transfer ALL the elements of 'array1' into 'array2' starting at array2[start]. An equivalent procedure is supplied for packing: PACK (array1,start,array2) will transfer the elements of 'array1' to all the elements of 'array2', starting with 'array1[start]'. For example, to UNPACK the array 'a' into the array 'b' use:

UNPACK(a,b,1)

and to repack

PACK(b,1,a)

The most important restriction encountered when using **PACKED ARRAY**s is that some versions of Pascal do not allow an element from a **PACKED ARRAY** to be used as the parameter for a function or procedure.

You may be thinking that this is a lot of fuss to make about the idea of **PACKED ARRAY**s but there is one type of **PACKED ARRAY** that is very important. The type

VAR variable:**PACKED ARRAY** [1..N] **OF** CHAR

is known as a string of length N. In the previous chapter on I/O we introduced the idea of a string being a collection of characters enclosed by single quotes, e.g. 'this is a string'. To be more accurate, N characters enclosed by single quotes is an example of a string constant of length N; i.e. 'this is a string' is a string constant of length 16. Following the rules about assigning entire arrays of the same type it should be clear that a string constant of length N can be assigned to a string variable of length N. For example:

```pascal
VAR name:PACKED ARRAY [1..5] OF CHAR;
BEGIN
        name:='FRED '
END
```

is a valid assignment of the constant 'FRED ' to the array 'name'. Notice that an extra blank must be included to make 'FRED' up to five letters, i.e. 'FRED '. Anywhere that a string constant can be used so can a string variable. For example, in WRITE('FRED ') we could use the string variable name to get WRITE(name), which would have the same effect. Notice that a string is the only type of array that can be used in its entirety in a WRITE statement. The individual elements of a string can be handled in exactly the same way as any other array. For example:

```pascal
PROGRAM namread(INPUT,OUTPUT);
VAR name: PACKED ARRAY [1..10] OF CHAR;
    ch:CHAR;
    i:INTEGER;
BEGIN
        FOR i:=1 TO 10 DO name[i]:=' ';
        i:=1;
        WHILE (NOT EOLN) AND (i=<10) DO
                BEGIN
                        READ(ch);
                        name[i]:=ch;
                        i:=i+1
                END;
        WRITELN(name)
END.
```

This program will read in a word with up to ten letters and will then write it out. The word is entered character by character and is terminated with an end of line character, i.e. carriage return. Notice the use of **NOT** EOLN to finish the **WHILE** statement if the end of line key is pressed, and the i=<10 condition to stop it if more than 10 characters are entered. Each character in the string is read in one element at a time but the entire string is then printed out using WRITELN(name).

Strings are so important that the relational operators have been extended to cover conditional expressions involving strings of the same length. The value of a conditional expression is worked out in such a way that strings are ordered in the same way as in a dictionary—so-called lexographic order. The result of a comparison between two strings of the same length is, in effect, the same as a

110

comparison made between the first pair of different characters (taken as type CHAR). For example: 'ABCD'<'ABCE' is true because the first pair of characters that are different is 'D' and 'E' and 'D'<'E' is true for CHAR. 'BAA'>'CAA' is also true because the first pair of characters that are different is 'B' and 'A' and 'B'>'A' is true for CHAR.

A typical use of strings and string conditional expressions is in the processing of answers to questions. For example:

```
PROGRAM quest(INPUT,OUTPUT);
VAR ans:PACKED ARRAY [1..3] OF CHAR;
     ch:CHAR;
     i:INTEGER;
BEGIN
     WRITELN;
     WRITE('is the area of a circle given by pi*r*r');
     i:=1;
     WHILE (NOT EOLN) AND (i<=3) DO
                    BEGIN
                              READ(ch);ans[i]:=ch;i=i+1
                    END;
     WRITELN;
     IF ans='yes' THEN WRITE('correct')
              ELSE WRITE('incorrect')
END.
```

When the program is run the question in the first WRITE appears on the screen. The answer 'yes' or 'no' can then be typed at the keyboard. If you want the answer 'y' to be treated as the same as 'yes' then replace the IF statement by:

```
IF ans[1]='y' THEN WRITE('correct') ELSE
WRITE('incorrect')
```

One annoying feature of standard Pascal strings is that they are of fixed length. This forces blanks to be written to make constants the same length as string variables. Some versions of Pascal, e.g. UCSD Pascal, supply yet another standard data type STRING that allows variable length strings to be used. This topic is too specialised to be covered in detail here. In any case, use of this facility should be avoided if you want your Pascal programs to run on other machines.

Arrays of arrays—multi-dimensional arrays

There is nothing to stop the type of the elements of an array themselves being arrays. For example:

VAR table:**ARRAY** [1..10] OF **ARRAY** [1..10] **OF**
INTEGERS;

defines 'table' to be an array of arrays! Each element of 'table' is itself an array, so 'table[1]' is an array of ten integer variables. You can use a second index to select one of the elements of the component arrays: i.e. 'table [1] [4]' is not an array but the fourth INTEGER element of the first array.

The use of arrays of arrays is so common that Pascal allows a short form of the definition:

VAR variable:**ARRAY** [type1,type2] **OF** type3

where 'type1' and 'type2' are types of the first and second index and 'type3' is the type of the elements of the array. For example, the array 'table' could have been defined by:

VAR table:**ARRAY** [1..10,1..10] **OF** INTEGER

A shorter form of selecting a particular INTEGER element is also allowed. Instead of 'table[i][j]' you can write 'table[i,j]'.

An array with two index variables is very often called a two-dimensional array because it is similar to a table of numbers. One of the index variables selects the row and the other the column in the table that contains the required information.

It is important to realise that the type of the two index variables do not have to be the same. For example:

TYPE day=(mon,tue,wed,thur,fri,sat,sun);
VAR timetab:**ARRAY** [day,1..5] **OF** INTEGER

'timetab' is a two-dimensional array suitable for storing the times of five trains that run every day of the week. The time of the second train on Tuesday would be stored in the INTEGER variable 'timetab[tue,2]'.

Arrays are not even restricted to two index variables. You can define an array of arrays of arrays and so on! In general these are referred to as multi-dimensional arrays. Any particular array is called n-dimensional if it has a maximum of n index variables, i.e. two index variables, two dimensions; three index variables, three dimensions, and so on. The shortened form of defining a two-dimensional array can be extended to any number of dimensions:

VAR variable:**ARRAY** [type1,type2,type3 ....] **OF** element type

The shortened form of referencing an array element can also be used.

variable[index1,index2,index3....]

112

The array is such a useful data structure that it is difficult to give a total picture of the ways that they are used. Some examples of programs that use arrays can be found in Chapter 11 but some of the more important and typical applications will be discussed in this section.

Any time that a list of any data type needs to be kept in such a way that access to any item in any order is required an array should be used. Sorting data is a typical application of this type. The data is read into an array and is then moved about until it is in order.

Arrays are also associated with two mathematical objects. The one-dimensional array corresponds to a vector and the two-dimensional array corresponds to a matrix. Obviously any program that has to carry out mathematical operations on vectors or matrices would make use of arrays.

Finally arrays can be used as look-up tables. The term look-up comes from the way the table is used to look up information. An example of a look-up table is a railway timetable.

A final comment on the use of arrays is that, although arrays cannot be used in WRITE and READ to text files, there is nothing wrong with a **FILE OF ARRAY**, etc. This means that there are two ways of using arrays and files. You can READ and WRITE single array elements of the correct type from text files, or entire arrays from files of arrays!

The RECORD

The **RECORD** is similar to **ARRAY** in that it is a collection of simpler data types under one name. The difference is that in the **ARRAY** each element had to be of the same type but in the **RECORD** you can use different types.

As an example of a **RECORD** consider an entry in a telephone directory consisting of a name and the number of a telephone extension. The obvious thing to do is to define a string or an array of characters for the name and an INTEGER for the number:

VAR name:**PACKED ARRAY** [1..10] **OF** CHAR;
       number:INTEGER;

Now although this pair of variables could be used in a telephone directory program, just as in the case of the data type **ARRAY**, it would be nice if we could define a single structured variable, say 'entry', which consisted of both pieces of information but which could be manipulated as if it was one. It is clear that there is no way that we can define an array with name and number as two elements but we can define a Pascal **RECORD**:

```
VAR entry:RECORD
               name:PACKED ARRAY [1..10] OF CHAR;
               number:INTEGER
          END
```

This defines the variable entry as a **RECORD** with two 'fields'. The first is 'name', a string variable of 10 letters, and the second is 'number', an INTEGER.

Access to the different fields of a record is made by using both the **RECORD**'s name and the field name, separated by a dot. For example:

```
entry.name:='Fred      ';
entry.number:=233
```

assign values to both fields.

The general form of a **RECORD** definition is:

```
VAR variable:RECORD
               identifier:type;
               identifier:type;
               identifier:type;

                  .     .     .

                  .     .     .

               identifier:type;
          END;
```

where 'identifier' is the name of the field and 'type' is the type of the field. 'Type' can be any valid Pascal type including another **RECORD**.

It is more usual to define **RECORD**s using the two steps of a **TYPE** statement and then a **VAR** statement. The reason for this is that **RECORD** definitions are normally long and it is better to define a type identifier for later use. For example:

```
TYPE tele=RECORD
               name:PACKED ARRAY [1..10] OF
               CHAR;
               number:INTEGER
          END;
VAR oldnum,newnum:tele
```

which defines both variables 'oldnum' and 'newnum' as **RECORD**s.

114

Although the components of a **RECORD** can be used as normal variables of their appropriate type (i.e. they can be combined in expressions, etc) the only operation that can be applied to a **RECORD** as a whole is assignment. Any **RECORD** can be assigned to another **RECORD** if the two are of identical type. For instance, if 'oldnum' and 'newnum' are **RECORD**s as defined in the last example:

```
oldnum:=newnum
```

would transfer all the fields in 'newnum' into 'oldnum'. That is,

```
oldnum.name:=newnum.name;
oldnum.number:=newnum.number
```

If a **RECORD** is used as a field of another **RECORD** then the field specification of any component of the inner **RECORD** is made up of all the identifiers associated with the component. It is easier to give an example rather than describe the general case. If we define a **RECORD** type called 'date',

```
TYPE date=RECORD
                date:1..31;
                mon:(jan,feb,mar,apr,may,jun,july,aug,
                    sept,oct,nov,dec);
                year:INTEGER
            END;
```

we can then define a **RECORD** suitable for storing some information about an order:

```
VAR order:RECORD
                orderno:INTEGER;
                dispatch:BOOLEAN;
                ordate:date
            END
```

The fields of the **RECORD** order are: 'order.orderno', 'order.dispatch' and 'order.ordate'. The first two are of type INTEGER and BOOLEAN respectively, but the third is also a **RECORD**. The fields of this **RECORD** can be specified by:

```
order.ordate.day
order.ordate.month
order.ordate.year
```

This idea of accumulating names can be extended to as many **RECORD**s as required.

As well as **RECORD**s and **ARRAY**s being used in **RECORD** definitions **RECORD**s can be used in other type definitions. For example, you can have **FILE OF RECORD**, and **ARRAY** [1..10] **OF RECORD**. The methods of accessing the individual components can then sometimes look confusing but they are always the simple application of the rules for each type separately. For example:

VAR birthday:**ARRAY** [1..5] **OF** date;

is an array of birthday dates. Each element of the array is a **RECORD** of type 'date' so, for example, 'birthday[2]' is a **RECORD**. Access to the particular fields of the **RECORD** is by the usual naming. Thus:

```
birthday[2].day
birthday[2].month
birthday[2].year
```

WITH *statement*

One of the problems of using **RECORD**s is that it can be very tedious to write out the full name of a field every time it is needed. Take the case of storing information in the **RECORD** 'order':

```
order.orderno:=345;
order.dispatch:=true;
order.ordate.day:=15;
order.ordate.mon:=feb;
order.ordate.year:=1982;
```

It would be nice if there was some way of leaving off the identifier 'order'. Unfortunately this would lead to confusion with any ordinary variables with the same name as the field. A solution is provided by the **WITH** statement whose general form is:

WITH recordvariable **DO** statement;

Where 'recordvariable' is the name of a **RECORD** and 'statement' is any Pascal statement. The effect of the **WITH** statement is to make any identifier that is the same as the name of a field of the **RECORD** refer to that field. This is easier to understand in an example:

```
WITH order DO
      BEGIN
              orderno:=345;
              dispatch:=true;
```

                    ordate.day:=15;
                    ordate.mon:=feb;
                    ordate.year:=1982
        END;

The list of assignments following the **DO** are equivalent to the previous assignments to the **RECORD** 'order'. Even if there was a simple
variable called 'orderno' the assignment following the **BEGIN** would
still use 'order.orderno'. It is possible to use **WITH** to specify more
than one **RECORD** name as default. For example:

  WITH order,ordate **DO**
                orderno:=345;
                dispatch:=true;
                day:=15;
                mon:=feb;
                year:=1982
        END;

which is again equivalent to the first set of assignments to 'order'.

Using **RECORD***s*

The **RECORD** type is very useful for any application where a traditional paper file would have been used to hold the information. The
fields of a Pascal record can be used in a similar way to the catego-
rised entries in card files, etc. This sort of application is typified by
the use of an external **FILE OF RECORD**. It is less obvious that
RECORDs can be used for more mathematical applications such as
providing a complex number type for Pascal:

  TYPE complex=**RECORD**
                re:REAL;
                im:REAL
        END

Of course, to make such a new type useful you could also have to
produce a set of functions and procedures to carry out the usual
operations of addition, multiplication, etc.

SETs

You may think that the previous two data types and their combina-
tions would be sufficient for every need. However, sometimes the
structured types **ARRAY** and **RECORD** impose too much struc-

ture on the underlying fundamental data types. The ordering that an **ARRAY** or **RECORD** implies can be unnecessary to store, for example, all the types of fruit in a fruit bowl. A **SET** is simply a collection of items with no order implied. Perhaps the best way to think of a **SET** is as a bag which may contain any number of items. In Pascal a **SET** constant is a list of items between square brackets. If we define, the type 'fruit' by

    TYPE fruit=(apple,orange,pear,banana)

then examples of valid **SET** constants are:

    [apple]
    [orange,apple,pear]
    [ ]

The first is the **SET** containing only 'apple', the second contains 'orange', 'apple' and 'pear', and the third **SET** contains nothing, i.e. it is empty. Notice that, as order is unimportant in **SET**s,

    [orange,apple,pear]

is the same as

    [apple,pear,orange]

Also, **SET**s that contain repeats of items are the same as if the item occurred only once. Thus:

    [apple,pear,apple]

is the same as

    [apple,pear]

You may feel that the first **SET** contains two apples and the second contains only one, but in this context 'apple' is a type of 'fruit' not an individual apple. Another way to look at this is that a **SET** records only the presence or absence of its elements. To avoid having to write out each item explicitly you can use the two-dot sub-range notation to mean all the items including and between the two items. For example:

    [orange..banana]

is the same as

    [orange,pear,banana]

and

    [apple..banana]

is the **SET** of all fruits.

118

As with constants of all data types it is possible to define variables that can be used to store them. A **SET** variable can be defined using:

VAR variable:**SET OF** type;

where 'type' is the type of the constants (and variables) that can make up the **SET**. Because of practical limitations 'type' must be either a subrange or a user-defined scalar type. For example, we could define a **SET** variable 'bowl' as

VAR bowl:**SET OF** fruit;

and some examples of valid assignments are:

```
bowl:=[apple,orange]
bowl:=[ ]
bowl:=[succ(orange),banana]
```

Notice that the third example uses an expression 'succ(orange)' to determine the constant that is in the **SET**, i.e. 'pear'.

There are three operations that can be used to manipulate **SET**s:

+　　**SET** union
*　　**SET** intersection
−　　**SET** difference

If 'a' and 'b' are two **SET**s of the same type then:

'a+b' evaluates to a **SET** that contains everything in **SET** 'a' and everything in **SET** 'b';

'a*b' evaluates to a **SET** that contains the things that 'a' and 'b' have in common;

'a−b' evaluates to a **SET** that contains everything in 'a' that is not in 'b'.

Some examples of **SET** expressions are:

```
[apple,pear]+[apple,banana] evaluates to [apple,pear,banana]
[apple,pear]*[apple,banana] evaluates to [apple]
[apple,pear]−[apple,banana] evaluates to [pear]
```

Conditional expression can also be formed using **SET**s, although the usual interpretations of the relational operators have to be abandoned and only four of them can be used:

=　　**SET** equality
<>　　**SET** inequality
<=　　**SET** inclusion
>=　　**SET** inclusion

If 'a' and 'b' are **SET**s of the same type then:

'a=b' is true if 'a' and 'b' contain exactly the same elements;
'a<>b' is true if '**NOT** (a=b)' is true;
'a<=b' is true if every element of 'b' is also in 'a';
'a>=b' is true if every element of 'a' is also in 'b'.

Some examples of **SET** conditional expressions are:

[apple,banana]=[banana,apple] is true
[apple,pear]<>[pear] is true
[apple,orange,pear]<=[banana] is false
[apple,orange]>=[banana,orange,apple] is true

All of the above four relational operators compare a **SET** with a **SET**. Pascal provides an additional relational operator, **IN**, that tests if an item is in a particular **SET**. The general form is:

expression **IN** set

The 'expression' must be of the same type as the elements of the set and the entire relational expression is true if the result of the expression is a member of the set. For example:

apple **IN** [pear,apple,orange] is true
succ(orange) **IN** [pear,apple,orange] is true
  (* note 'succ(orange)' is 'pear' *)
pear **IN** [apple,banana] is false

Notice that the item on the right of **IN** is not a set.

The use of **SET***s*

Operations involving **SET**s can very often be faster than using other structured types and so they should be used wherever it makes sense. The only trouble is that many versions of Pascal place a very low upper limit on the size of **SET**s that are allowed.

Two typical applications of **SET**s are for simplifying complex **IF** statements, for example:

IF (ans='y') **OR** (ans='a') **OR** (ans='c') **THEN** . . .

can be written

IF ans **IN** ['y','a','c'] **THEN** . . .

and for classifying types into subranges, for example:

number **IN** [0..10]

or

letter **IN** [a..z]

or

digit **IN** [0..9]

Apart from these two small uses, **SET**s do not appear very often in Pascal programs; this is possibly because **SET**s are the least familiar of all structured types. However, this should not stop you from exploring the possibility that a **SET** would suit your problem better.

Using structured types

In theory you should be able to use a structured type anywhere that its use would make sense. For example, you can most certainly define a **FILE** of any structured type. In particular **FILE**s of **ARRAY**s and of **RECORD**s can be used, and this in turn implies that GET and PUT can be used with structured types. The parameters of user-defined **FUNCTION**s and **PROCEDURE**s can also be structured types but many versions of Pascal place restrictions on exactly how structured types can be used in this context: most versions will not allow a function to return a structured value for example. To make the point clear, you can write things like:

FUNCTION sum(list:**ARRAY** [1..10] **OF** INTEGER)

in all but the most crude and restrictive versions of Pascal.

Summary

The idea of a structured type was dealt with in this chapter. In particular the three types **ARRAY**, **RECORD** and **SET** were discussed in detail.

Questions

1. Write definitions of **ARRAY**s suitable for storing:
    —the temperature of six different chemical baths;
    —the temperature of each day for a week;
    —someone's name;
    —the number of days in each month of the year.

2. Write definitions of **RECORD**s suitable for storing:
   —a person's name and date of birth;
   —a six-figure bank account number and the amount on deposit;
   —a weather record including rainfall, wind direction and speed.

3. Define a **SET** of colours suitable for storing the state of a three-colour traffic light and write down **SET**s that correspond to 'stop' and 'go'. What do you think that the empty **SET** might be used for in this case?

4. Write **FOR** statements that will zero all the elements of

VAR a:**ARRAY** [1..10,1..10] **OF** INTEGER

10
Practical Pascal—II

In this second chapter of example programs we focus on the full use of Pascal rather than on the process of writing programs. As a result of this shift of emphasis the intermediate steps in the production of the program are not given in full. The examples are all fairly simple to allow the details of the use of Pascal to be as clear as possible.

Printing BOOLEAN and user-defined types

Our first problem concerns the shortcomings of the supplied procedure WRITE, which will only accept a limited range of data types when working with text files. The reasons for this were explained in Chapter 8. In particular, you cannot use WRITE to print a user-defined scalar type and some versions of Pascal do not allow WRITE to be used to print a BOOLEAN type. It would obviously be useful to have a procedure that extended the range of I/O operations to these types.

For BOOLEAN this is a simple matter. The procedure 'writeb' given below can be included in any program and will write 'true' or 'false' according to the value of the BOOLEAN parameter.

```
PROCEDURE writeb(x:BOOLEAN);
BEGIN
        IF x THEN WRITE('true')
           ELSE WRITE('false')
END
```

Notice that 'x' is a value parameter, which allows 'writeb' to be used to print the result of a BOOLEAN expression, i.e. 'writeb(a AND b)' is valid.

The problem for a general user-defined scalar type is more complicated than BOOLEAN type. The difficulty is that there are likely to be more than just two values and we do not know in advance what names they might take. Consider the problem of writing a procedure that will print out the values taken by a variable or expression of the type 'day':

TYPE day=(mon,tue,wed,thur,fri,sat,sun)

The procedure given below solves this problem using a **CASE** statement.

```
PROCEDURE writeday(x:day);
BEGIN
        CASE x OF
                mon:WRITE('Monday');
                tue:WRITE('Tuesday');
                wed:WRITE('Wednesday');
                thur:WRITE('Thursday');
                fri:WRITE('Friday');
                sat:WRITE('Saturday');
                sun:WRITE('Sunday')
        END
END
```

As in the case of 'writeb' a value parameter is used to allow expressions as well as variables of the type 'day'. Notice that the words printed out are not the same as the value identifiers; for example, for the value 'sun' the word Sunday is printed. This is of course an optional improvement.

Formatted printing of REAL—an example of the WHILE statement

It is difficult to find a simple example of the use of the **WHILE** statement because most elementary problems involve carrying out part of a program a known number of times and this is better solved using the **FOR** statement. Consider however the problem of converting a real number greater than one to exponent form—like 3.24E+6, for instance.

This looks as if it might be a difficult problem but if you take any real number, 32.34 for example, it can be converted to the form by using a rule given in Chapter 3, where exponent form was introduced: if you move the decimal point one place to the left you must increase the exponent by one.

As moving the decimal point one place to the left corresponds to dividing by ten, a suitable solution is to divide the number by ten until it is smaller than one and, each time the number is divided by ten, one is added to the exponent. This could be written as a Pascal **PROCEDURE** as:

```
PROCEDURE  conexp(number:REAL;VAR  frac:REAL;VAR
exp:INTEGER);
```

BEGIN
        exp:=0;
        WHILE number>1.0 **DO**
                BEGIN
                        number:=number/10.0;
                        exp:=exp+1
                END;
        frac:=number
END

Notice the use of **WHILE** to repeat the division and exponent count **WHILE** number is greater than one. Another point worth noticing is the use of value and variable parameters in the **PROCEDURE**. The parameter 'number' is a value parameter for two reasons; first, it allows the results of expressions to be converted, e.g. conexp(3.2*pi,fl,el) is valid; and second, it allows 'number' to be used in the procedure without affecting any variables in the main program. If 'number' was a variable parameter the division

    number:=number/10.0

would alter a variable in the main program. The parameters 'exp' and 'frac' are defined as variable parameters because they are going to be used to return the results of the **PROCEDURE**.

For an example of the use of 'conexp' consider:

PROGRAM test(INPUT,OUTPUT);
VAR pi,fl:REAL;el:INTEGER;
    (include the definition of conexp here)
BEGIN
        pi:=3.14159;
        conexp(pi,fl,el);
        WRITELN;
        WRITELN(pi,fl:8:6,el:4)
END.

Notice the use of field specifications in the last WRITELN. The variable 'fl' is to be printed using eight characters, six of which should be after the decimal point. As 'fl' should contain a number less than one the first character will be zero, the next the decimal point and the rest will be the fractional part that we have calculated.

Bubble sort

A fairly common problem is to rearrange a list of numbers or letters into order. There are many ways of achieving this reordering but one of the easiest to understand is the so-called bubble sort. A bubble sort works by scanning through the list comparing adjacent items and swapping them if they are in the wrong order. Obviously, to achieve a complete reordering it is possible that a large number of scans will have to be made. If a complete scan of the list is made without any swaps occurring then the list must be in the correct order. Translating these ideas into Pascal is fairly straightforward. The list of numbers or letters can be represented by an **ARRAY** and the scan can be produced with a **FOR** statement. For example:

```
PROGRAM bub(INPUT,OUTPUT);
VAR temp:REAL;
        no, i:INTEGER;
      swap:BOOLEAN;
        list:ARRAY [1..20] OF INTEGER;
BEGIN
        WRITELN;WRITE('number of items =');
        READ(no);WRITELN;
        FOR i:=1 TO no DO
                BEGIN
                        WRITE('item ',i,' = ');
                        READ(list[i]);
                        WRITELN
                END;
(* begin sort*)

        swap:=true;
        WHILE swap DO
(* scan list *)
        BEGIN
                swap:=false;
                FOR i:=1 TO no−1 DO
                                IF list[i]<list[i+1] THEN
                                BEGIN
                                    temp:=list[i+1];
                                    list[i+1]:=list[i];
                                    list[i]:=temp;
                                    swap:=true
                                END
        END;
(* print the sorted list *)
        WRITELN;
        FOR i:=1 TO no DO WRITE(list[i])
END.
```

The points to notice about this program are the use of 'swap' to record the fact that a swap has occurred, the fact that the **FOR** statement stops at 'no−1' and the way 'temp' is used to swap 'list[i]' with 'list[i+1]'.

It is important to realise and remember that, although sorting is easy to understand using the bubble sort method, there are much better and faster methods available.

A draughts board

This example is incomplete in the sense that it forms the starting point for a more complicated program. The problem is to set up the normal starting arrangement of pieces for a game of draughts or checkers. The representation of the board by an 8 by 8 array is obvious. However, the data type used to represent the pieces is less easily decided. Each square on the board must be in one of four conditions:

   —occupied by a white piece
   —occupied by a black piece
   —empty and white
   —empty and black.

So it would make sense to define a scalar with values '(black, white,bpiece,wpiece)'. The final data definition is:

TYPE squares=(black,white,bpiece,wpiece);
VAR board:**ARRAY** [1..8,1..8] **OF** squares

The final and most difficult problem is that of assigning the correct values to each element of the **ARRAY**. If the top left-hand corner of the board corresponds to 'board[1,1]', and the first index corresponds to the row number and the second corresponds to the column number, then the following are true:

   —in an odd-numbered row the odd columns are black
   —in an even-numbered row the even columns are black.

For example, 'board[1,1]' is black because it is in an odd row and column, but 'board[2,1]' is white because it is in an even row but an odd column. To find out the colour of any square we can use the rule: board[row,col] is black, if row and col are both even or both odd, and is white otherwise. This rule is easy to implement in Pascal because of the supplied BOOLEAN function ODD. If 'var' is odd the value of 'ODD(var)' is true.

Once we have assigned colours to all the squares, the problem of setting up the initial positions of all the pieces is easy: the first two rows' white squares are changed to 'wpiece' and the last two rows' white squares are changed to 'bpiece'. The final program is:

```
PROGRAM draughts(INPUT,OUTPUT);
TYPE squares=(black,white,bpiece,wpiece);
VAR board:ARRAY [1..8,1..8] OF squares;
    row,col:INTEGER;
BEGIN
      FOR row:=1 TO 8 DO
          FOR col:=1 TO 8 DO
                IF ODD(row) AND ODD(col)
                      THEN board[row,col]:=black
                      ELSE board[row,col]:=white;
(* set up pieces *)
      FOR row:=1 TO 2 DO
          FOR col:=1 TO 8 DO
                IF board[row,col]=white
                      THEN board[row,col]:=bpiece;
      FOR row:=7 TO 8 DO
          FOR col:=1 TO 8 DO
                IF board[row,col]=white
                      THEN board[row,col]:=wpiece
END.
```

The interesting points to notice are the use of nested **FOR** loops to
scan the array and the way the **IF** statement is used to set the
colours.

This program could be improved by the reader to include a suitable printout of the board. Ambitious readers may feel like taking on
the challenge of reading in and making moves and even making the
computer play as an opponent!

Telephone directory—an example of RECORD handling

It is difficult to give a short example that shows the power of the
data type **FILE OF RECORD**. This example of a telephone directory serves to illustrate the ideas involved in **RECORD** and **FILE**
handling and provides the basis for further development.

There are two parts to the problem of producing a usable telephone directory:

    —creating and maintaining the directory

    —interrogating the directory.

The first part of the problem can be treated most simply if we make
the unrealistic assumption that the list of phone numbers will be
entered just once and never updated. In this case a directory creation program would look something like:

```pascal
PROGRAM create(INPUT,OUTPUT,direc);
TYPE digit='0'..'9';
        entry=RECORD name:ARRAY [1..20] OF CHAR;
                      number:ARRAY [1..7] OF DIGIT;
              END;
VAR ok:BOOLEAN;
    i,j:INTEGER;
    ans:CHAR;
    direc:FILE OF entry;
    person:entry;
BEGIN
        rewrite(direc); (*initialise file*)
        FOR j:=1 TO 15 DO (*read in 15 records*)
              BEGIN
                  FOR i:=1 TO 20 DO person.name[i]=' ';
                  ok:=false;
                  WHILE NOT ok DO
                          BEGIN
                                      (* read in name *)
                                      WRITELN;
                                      WRITE('First name = ');
                                      i:=1;
                                      WHILE NOT EOLN DO
                                              BEGIN

                                      READ(person.name[i]);
                                              i:=i+1
                                          END;
                                      (*readin number*)
                                      WRITELN;

                                      WRITE('Telephone
                                      number= ');
                                      FOR i:=1 TO 7 DO
                                          READ(person.number[i]);
                                      WRITELN;
                                      (* entry ok? *)
                                      WRITE('is the entry ok ?
                                      y/n');
                                      READ(ans);
                                      ok:=ans='y';
                          END;
                  (*write the record out*)
```

```
                direc^:=person;
                PUT(direc)
        END
END.
```

This program is far from perfect but it does show some basic file and record-handling methods. Among its weaknesses are that only a file with 15 entries can be constructed, that each number must have seven digits and that any mistakes in entering part of the record can only be corrected by re-entering the whole record.

Once the telephone directory file has been constructed we can use it to look up somene's telephone number. This is most easily done by reading through the file until we have a match for the person's name. A suitable look-up program would be something like:

```
PROGRAM getnum(INPUT,OUTPUT,direc);
TYPE digit='0'..'9';
        entry=RECORD name:ARRAY [1..20] OF CHAR;
                     number:ARRAY [1..7] OF DIGIT;
              END;
VAR i:INTEGER;
    ans:CHAR;
    more,found:BOOLEAN;
    name:ARRAY [1..20] OF CHAR;
    direc:FILE OF entry;
    person:entry;
BEGIN
        WRITELN;
        more:=true;
        WHILE more DO
                BEGIN
                        WRITELN;
                        FOR i:=1 TO 20 DO name[i]:=" ";
                        i:=0;
                        WRITE('last name = ');
                        WHILE NOT EOLN DO
                                BEGIN
                                        READ(name[i]);
                                        i:=i+1
                                END;
                        (* find name in file *)
                        reset(direc);
                        found:=false;
                        WHILE (NOT EOF (direc)) AND
                              (NOT found) DO
```

```
                    BEGIN
                        found:=true;
                        FOR i:=1 TO 20 DO
                          IF direc^.name[i]<>name[i]
                            THEN found:=false;
                        IF NOT found THEN
                        get(direc);
                    END;
                IF EOF (direc) THEN WRITELN
                              ('no such name
                              in directory')
                        ELSE FOR i:=1 TO 7
                        DO
                            WRITELN(direc^.
                            number[i]);
        WRITELN('do you want to look up another number
        y/n');
        READ(ans);
        more:=ans=y
        END
    END.
```

Notice the way the variables 'more' and 'found' are used to indicate that another number is required and that the name has been found.

Letter use—an example of SET

The simple problem of listing all the letters used in a sentence provides a situation where a **SET** can be used to advantage. The idea behind the solution is simply to build up a **SET** containing all the letters in the sentence and then go through the alphabet testing each letter to see if it is **IN** the **SET**.

```
PROGRAM letcount(INPUT,OUTPUT);
TYPE upper='A'..'Z';
VAR letter:upper;
    used:SET OF upper;
BEGIN
    used:=[];
    (*Read in each letter of sentence and add to SET*)
    WRITELN;
    WHILE NOT EOLN DO
```

```
        BEGIN
            READ(letter);
            used:=used+[letter]
        END;
    WRITELN;
    (*print out each letter used*)
    FOR letter:='A' TO 'Z' DO
            IF letter IN used THEN WRITELN(letter)
END.
```

The interesting features of this program include the use of a **FOR** statement with an index of type 'upper' and the set operators '+' (union) and **IN**.

Summary

Examples covering a number of areas of Pascal have been described.

Questions

1. Write a program to read in values of the data type 'day' defined in the second example in this chapter.

2. Write a version of 'conexp' that will convert numbers smaller than one into exponent form.

3. Write a **PROCEDURE** to initialise the draughts board to black and white squares.

4. Write a version of the 'letcount' program that will also count the number of times each letter is used.

11
Some advanced features

In this chapter some areas are introduced that are best left until you are interested in taking your understanding of Pascal further. Although the chapter has the word advanced in its title the topics covered are not difficult to understand. Two new control statements are introduced—**REPEAT-UNTIL** and **GOTO**—along with two extra data types, the variant **RECORD** and pointer types. The two control statements are not necessary for good Pascal programming and indeed the use of the **GOTO** is to be positively avoided! However, they are worth knowing about if only to be able to read other people's programs. The two data types are very definitely useful in their own right but are fairly specialised.

REPEAT-UNTIL

The **REPEAT-UNTIL** statement is superficially very similar to the **WHILE** statement but it is very important to be aware of the ways in which it differs. The general form of the **REPEAT-UNTIL** is:

REPEAT
         list of Pascal statements
UNTIL   boolean expression

where 'list of Pascal statements' is any list of valid Pascal statements separated by semicolons. The 'list' is carried out repeatedly until the BOOLEAN expression evaluates to true. When the **REPEAT** is encountered during normal program execution control carries on unaffected, i.e. the 'list of statements' is executed. When the **UNTIL** is encountered the BOOLEAN expression is evaluated. If it evaluates to true then control passes to the next statement. If it evaluates to false then control is diverted back to the first statement in the 'list'. For example:

i:=0;
REPEAT

```
            WRITELN(i);
            i:=i+1
   UNTIL    i=10
```

will print zero to nine. Notice that the final value of 'i' (i.e. 10) isn't printed out because this value causes the BOOLEAN expression to evaluate to true and control passes out of the loop.

The **REPEAT** statement differs from **WHILE** in that the 'list of statements' is carried out at least once (because the test occurs at the end of the loop). For example:

```
   i:=0;
   WHILE i<>0 DO WRITE(i);
```

will not print the value of 'i', but

```
   i:=0
   REPEAT
            WRITE(i)
   UNTIL    i=0
```

will. Notice that the BOOLEAN expression in the **WHILE** is the 'not' of the BOOLEAN expression in the **REPEAT**. This is because the **WHILE** requires the expression to be true for the loop to continue, **REPEAT** requires the expression to be true for the loop to END. Another difference is that the **REPEAT** statement doesn't require the 'list of statements' to be enclosed by a **BEGIN** and **END**. In this respect it is different from every other Pascal control statement and because of this some people include an unnecessary **BEGIN** and **END**.

It is easy to decide if a **REPEAT** statement is the type of loop that you need. Simply ask yourself the question, 'Do I want the loop to be carried out at least once?' If the answer is yes then it is probable that a **REPEAT** loop will make your program shorter and easier to understand.

GOTO

The range of statements that alter the flow of control—**IF, CASE, FOR, WHILE** and now **REPEAT**— are very precise in the way that they work. Using them we can select among a number of options (**IF** and **CASE**) or repeat a block of program (**FOR, WHILE** and **REPEAT**). It can be shown that these two actions of selection and repetition are all that are required to write any program!

Although this is true there are times when the ability to force the transfer of control from one part of a program to another would be very useful, for example if at some point early on in a program an error condition was detected that was so serious that the rest of the program should not be carried out. So far the only way that we can avoid carrying out the rest of the program is to include tests on a BOOLEAN variable that is made true if an error has occurred. In some ways it would be easier if we could give a command something like 'go to the end of the program' when the error was found.

Pascal does include such a statement—the **GOTO** statement—but before we can define it we first have to consider how to mark the point in the program that control is going to pass to. For this purpose Pascal allows the definition of labels. A label is an unsigned whole number with at most four digits. Any labels that are going to be used in the body of a program must be defined before anything else, i.e. before constants, new types, variables or procedures/functions. A label is defined by:

LABEL label list;

where 'label list' is a list of labels separated by commas. For example:

LABEL 23,43,1,2,9999;

Any statement in a program can be marked by prefixing it with a label and a colon. For example:

```
23:i:=i+1;
43:IF i=4 THEN . . .
```

Notice that only one statement can be marked with each label defined and the numerical value of a label has no meaning.

The general form of the **GOTO** is:

GOTO label

where 'label' has been defined previously. The effect of such a statement is to transfer control to the statement marked by the label. For example,

GOTO 23

would transfer control to the statement marked by the label 23. If the label used by a **GOTO** either has not been defined or not been used to mark a statement then an error occurs. If you transfer control into a statement that is part of another control statement, for example a **FOR** loop, then strange things can happen! For example,

```
FOR i:=1 TO 10 DO
    BEGIN
            j:=i*2;
        23:WRITELN(i)
    END;
  GOTO 23
```

may not be rejected as an error by your version of Pascal but it is
most certainly wrong!

The **GOTO** statement should only be used to deal with situations
that are not really part of the normal running of a program. If you
find that you are using **GOTO** rather a lot when you write your own
programs then this is most probably a sign that you are not really
getting the most out of Pascal.

Variant **RECORDs**

The data type **RECORD** is probably the most useful data structure
that Pascal can offer for solving commercial or data processing problems. The reason for this is that it is usually possible to define a
RECORD with fields that correspond to items that would appear on
a traditional card record. There is however one situation that is easy
to handle when using a written card record that the simple Pascal
RECORD cannot cope with. Consider the problem of keeping an
employment record. The fields might be name, sex, age and job
status. So far we can define a **RECORD** capable of holding this
information in the usual way:

```
TYPE jobstat=(emp,unemp);
     emprec=RECORD
                name:PACKED ARRAY [1..20] OF
                  CHAR;
                sex:(male,female);
                age:(15..65);
                job:jobstat
            END
```

The trouble with this **RECORD** becomes clear when we try to store
information following the 'job' field if what we want to record
depends on the value that the 'job' field takes. If the person is
employed then we want to record the name of the employer, but if
the person is unemployed we want to record the date of their last
employment. To allow for this difference in structure depending on

136

the value of a field. Pascal provides the variant **RECORD**. The easiest way to explain the variant **RECORD** is by an example. The employment **RECORD** defined above would be, as a variant **RECORD**,

```
TYPE jobstat=(emp,unemp);
     date=ARRAY [1..3] OF INTEGER;
     emprec=RECORD
               name:PACKED ARRAY [1..20] OF CHAR;
               sex:(male,female);
               age:(15..65);
               CASE job:jobstat OF
                   emp:(employer:PACKED ARRAY [1..20]
                   OF CHAR);
                   unemp:(lastemp:date)
          END
```

The definition of the **RECORD** 'emprec' now falls into two parts. The part from **RECORD** to **CASE** doesn't depend on the value of any field and is therefore called the fixed part. The part from **CASE** to **END** does depend on the value of the field 'job' and is known as the variant part. The field 'job' is known as a tag field. If the value of 'job' is 'emp' then the **RECORD** has a field called 'employer' of type **PACKED ARRAY**. If the value of 'job' is 'unemp' then the **RECORD** has a field called 'lastemp' of type 'date'. Assuming the definition:

```
VAR rec1:emprec
```

then the following assignments are valid:

```
rec1.job:=emp;rec1.employer:="acme chemical co  "
```

or

```
rec1.job:=unemp:rec1.lastemp[1]:=6;
rec1.lastemp[2]:=5;rec1.lastemp[3]:=82;
```

Trying to assign data to a field that does not exist when the tag field has a particular value causes an error. For example,

```
rec1.job:=emp;rec1.lastemp[1]:=5;
```

is incorrect because the field 'lastemp' does not exist for the tag field value assigned.

The general form of a variant **RECORD** is,

        CASE tagfieldname:type **OF**
                tagvaluelist:(field list);

                        .   .   .

                        .   .   .

                tagvaluelist:(field list);
        END

where 'tagvaluelist' is a list of values separated by commas that the
tag field can take, and the 'field list' is a list of field definitions that
apply when the tag field is one of the values in the 'tagvaluelist'. It is
possible that for some tag field values there are no extra fields. This
is indicated by an empty pair of brackets (). There are two points to
notice about variant **RECORD**s: first, all field names must be distinct even if they occur in different variants; second, a **RECORD**
can have only one variant part, although the variant part can contain variant **RECORD**s.

As another example of a variant **RECORD** consider the problem
of recording some information about car ownership. We might use
the following **RECORD** for the purpose:

        TYPE vehicle=(none,car,van,lorry,estate);
                regno=**PACKED ARRAY** [1..7] **OF** CHAR;
                RECORD
                        name:**PACKED ARRAY** [1..20] **OF** CHAR;
                        CASE drives:vehicle **OF**
                        none:();
                        car,estate:(passno:1..5);
                        van,lorry:(weight:1..20)
        END

If the tag field 'vehicle' is 'none' then there are no other fields in the
RECORD. If the tag field is either 'car' or 'estate' then there is a
field to record the number of passengers and if the tag field is either
'van' or 'lorry' then there is a field to record the weight. Notice that
it is entirely up to the programmer to try to avoid making assignments to fields that do not exist for a given value of the tag field.
Because of this extra burden the use of variant **RECORD**s is likely
to make a program more difficult to get working reliably.

Pointer type

All of the variables that we have used so far have been static in the
sense that their number has been fixed before the program is run.
There is the facility within Pascal to create new variables as a program is running but this involves the introduction of a number of

138

extra ideas. The first difference between the static variables that we have been used to and these new dynamic variables is that they are not referred to by a name (an identifier) but via a new data type—pointer. A variable of type pointer does not store any data but instead is used to hold the whereabouts of another variable. Thus a pointer variable can be thought of as pointing to another variable. It sometimes helps to imagine a pointer variable as actually having an arrow pointing to the un-named variable—as below:

pointer—————————————→variable

This idea is easier to understand after the formal definition and introduction of pointer types. A pointer type is defined by an upward arrow ^ written in front of the name of another data type. For example:

VAR a:^INTEGER

defines 'a' to be a variable of pointer type. The type that comes after the arrow in the definition of a pointer type is the only data type that the pointer can be used with. In this case the variable 'a' can only be used to point to INTEGER variables. Pointer types are said to be bound to the type that they can be used with—thus 'a' is bound to INTEGER type.

When a pointer type is first defined it is initialised to a special value 'nil'. The value 'nil' means that a pointer isn't pointing at any variable. To make a pointer point at a variable we must use the supplied procedure NEW. The statement NEW(pointer) does two things: first, it creates a variable of the type that the pointer is bound to; and second, it makes the pointer point at the newly created variable. The newly created variable is different from any type of variable that we have met so far in that it does not have a name but it is the same in all other respects. For example, NEW(a) creates a variable of type INTEGER and makes 'a' point at it. It is important to note that every time NEW is used a brand-new variable that is completely distinct from any others is brought into being.

You should now be able to see why the variables created by NEW are called dynamic: by repeated use of NEW you can create as many variables as required while the program is running. Some versions of Pascal also supply a function DISPOSE(pointer) that will destroy the variable that the pointer points at.

The only operations allowed on pointer variables are assignment and testing for equality or inequality. As an example of the use of pointer variables consider the following:

```
VAR a,b:^INTEGER;
BEGIN
        IF a=nil THEN NEW(a);
        b:=a
END
```

The variables 'a' and 'b' are defined to be pointers bound to INTEGER. The **IF** statement tests to see if 'a' is already pointing at a variable; if it isn't then NEW is used to create a variable of type INTEGER and make 'a' point at it. The assignment b:=a then makes 'b' point at the same INTEGER variable as 'a'. In terms of the arrow diagram this program can be visualised as:

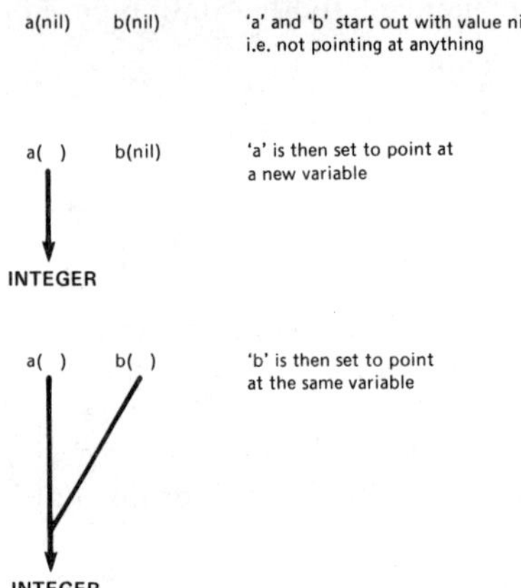

The key to understanding the manipulation of pointer variables is always to remember that you are assigning or comparing pointers to other variables. This is all very well but so far we have no way of assigning values to the variables that pointer types point to! The solution to this problem is simple. Writing an upward arrow to the right of a pointer variable is taken to mean 'the variable that the pointer is pointing at'. For example, 'a' is a pointer variable but 'a^' is the INTEGER that 'a' is pointing at.

```
a:=34  is incorrect because 'a' is
          a pointer and 34 is an
          INTEGER
a^:=34 is correct and 34 is
          assigned to the variable
          that 'a' points at.
```

Notice that the arrow is written to the left when defining the pointer

140

but to the right when using the variable that the pointer points at. It is important that the difference between

    a:=b

and

    a^:=b^

is clearly understood. The assignment a:=b sets the pointer 'a' to POINT at the SAME variable as pointer 'b'. But the assignment a^:=b^ copies the value stored in the variable pointed at by 'b' into the different variable pointed at by 'a'.

As a simple example of the use of pointers consider the following problem. Two sections of a factory make two different products from the same five parts. The difficulty is that each section has its own serial number for the same part. So, for example, what section one calls part number one, section two calls part number three, etc. A common stock control department is set up and is faced with the problem of keeping track of the numbers of each part in stock.

One solution would be to set up two INTEGER **ARRAY**s containing the number of parts in stock for each section. However, if a shipment of the part that section one calls part number one arrives, the total number of parts of what section two calls part three also has to be updated. In short, any change in the total quantity of any of section one's part number must also be carried out on the equivalent part for section two. The problem is obviously that each part has two names but only one value indicating the number in stock.

A better solution would be to set up two **ARRAY**s of pointers. Each pointer would point to a variable of type INTEGER used to hold the number in stock of the corresponding part. By allowing a pointer in each array to point to a common variable we can mirror the real world, i.e. one value for the number in stock but two pointers (names). The resulting program would be something like:

```
PROGRAM stock(INPUT,OUTPUT);
TYPE part=^INTEGER;
VAR secone,sectwo:ARRAY [1..50] OF part;
      i,num:INTEGER;
BEGIN
          (* create INTEGER variables *)
          FOR i:=1 TO 5 DO NEW(secone[i]);
          (* set up section two's pointers *)
          sectwo[3]:=secone[1];
          sectwo[2]:=secone[2];
          sectwo[4]:=secone[3];
```

```
            sectwo[5]:=secone[4];
            sectwo[1]:=secone[5];
            (* read in stock levels *)
            FOR i:=1 TO 5 DO
              BEGIN
                        WRITE(' Number in stock of part no ',i);
                        READ(num);
                        secone[i]^:=num
              END;
            (* write out stock levels for both departments *)
            FOR i:=1 TO 5 DO
              BEGIN
                num:=secone[i]^;
                WRITELN('Section one part no',i,'=',num);
              END;
            WRITELN
            FOR i:=1 TO 5 DO
              BEGIN
                num:=sectwo[i]^;
                WRITELN('Section two part no',i,'=',num)
              END;
    END.
```

This program by no means handles stock control, it simply illustrates the idea of using pointer type. Notice that each pointer in 'secone' is made to point at a new INTEGER variable. The pointers in 'sectwo' are set to point at the same INTEGER variables as 'secone'. For example, 'secone[1]' and 'sectwo[3]' point at the same variable. As a result of sharing the same variables, the stock totals only have to be read in once, for 'secone', and they assume the correct values for 'sectwo'.

Although the procedure NEW can create new variables, at the moment the number of variables that can be used is limited by the number of pointer variables defined in the program. For example, NEW(a) creates a variable that 'a' points at and another use of NEW(a) creates yet another variable that 'a' points at. The trouble is that unless we have assigned 'a' to another pointer before the second NEW(a) the first variable created is lost for ever because we have no way of referring to it. We could overcome this problem of a limited number of pointer types if the variable created by NEW in some way included another pointer type! This is possible if the pointer type is bound to a **RECORD** with a field of pointer type. For example:

TYPE link=ˆitem;
      item=**RECORD**
            value:INTEGER;
            next:link
        END;
 VAR first:link

This **TYPE** statement defines link to be a pointer type bound to 'item', a **RECORD**. The **VAR** statement defines 'first' to be of type 'link' so the statement NEW(first) creates a new variable that is a **RECORD** of type 'item'. As always, the pointer 'first' is set to point at this **RECORD** so assignment statements such as

firstˆ.value:=232

are valid. The definition of the **RECORD** type 'item' includes a field 'next' which is also a pointer. This means that every time we use NEW(first) we create an extra pointer variable as a field of the **RECORD**.

The only question that remains is how can we use these extra pointer variables to keep track of new **RECORD**s as they are created? The full answer to this question is beyond the scope of this book but the simplest method is to create a so-called linked list. A linked list is best understood via a diagram:

start———→item.next———→item.next———→item.next(nil)

In other words we use a pointer called 'start' to point at the latest version of the variable and use pointer field 'item.next' to point to the previous version of the variable. The variable that 'start' points at is said to be at the head of the list. A program to create such a linked list would be something like:

```
PROGRAM list(INPUT,OUTPUT);
TYPE link=ˆitem;
     item=RECORD
                  value:INTEGER;
                  next:link
            END
VAR first,current:link;
BEGIN
        (*create first record*)
        NEW(current);
        (*set next to nil to indicate end of list*)
        currentˆ.next:=nil;
        (* set first to point at current*)
        first:=current;
        (*now create another record*)
```

        NEW(current);
        (*set next to point at the previous head of list*)
        current^.next:=first;
        (*and update first to point to current record*)
        first:=current;

and so on.

The best way to understand this program is to consider the action of adding a single **RECORD** to the list. The pointer 'start' points to the first **RECORD** in the list. A new variable is created by NEW (current). To insert this new variable into the list requires two changes to the pointers. First, the newly created **RECORD** must be set to point at the head of the list. This is achieved by:

    current^.next:=start

Second, the pointer 'first' must be set to point at the newly created variable, thus making it the new head of the list. This is achieved by:

    start:=current

Obviously, any program that makes use of a linked list would also store information in other fields of the **RECORD**s as they are created. Once a linked list has been created it can be searched and modified by using the sequence of pointers. The details are not difficult but would take a lot of space to illustrate.

The purpose of this section has been to give some idea of the sorts of things for which pointer variables can be used. Pointer types and dynamic variables need a knowledge of computers that goes beyond PASCAL before they can be put to good use. However, if you are interested in programming, pointer types are too good to be avoided for long!

Summary

In this chapter four new topics were discussed: **REPEAT-UNTIL**, **GOTO**, variant **RECORD**s and pointer types. **REPEAT** and **GOTO** are two extra control statements that are available in PASCAL but neither is necessary to the writing of good programs. In fact the use of **GOTO** is to be avoided if at all possible. Variant **RECORD**s and pointer types further enrich the range of data types that can be used to construct programs. Variant **RECORD**s have a fairly well-defined application where a fixed **RECORD** is not flexible enough. However, the range of applications of pointer types is far less well defined and hence much greater. Pointer types can be used

144

to make a very wide range of dynamic types but the responsibility
for creation and manipulation is entirely with the programmer.

Questions

1. Write a program that asks a question to which the only acceptable
answers are yes or no. Use a **REPEAT-UNTIL** to repeat the question until the user answers yes or no.

2. Define a variant **RECORD** suitable for storing the following
information:
    —age
    —marital status
    —if married—spouse's name
              —time since marriage
    —if single   —name of next of kin

3. Write sample assignment statements for the **RECORD** defined in
question 2 for both a single and a married person.

12
Describing Pascal

There is a problem in describing Pascal, or any other language for that matter. It is easy to write down an example of a statement from the language but it is very difficult to define in general terms the overall look of all possible statements of the type. So, although when discussing the **VAR** statement it is easy to write an example:

   VAR total,sum:INTEGER

it is very difficult to describe all the possible variations that are allowed. If we write something like

   VAR variable name :data type

as a definition of the general **VAR** statement then we are relying on prior understanding that 'variable name' and 'data type' are to be replaced in any actual **VAR** statement by a real variable name and an actual data type. It is important to distinguish in the definition those parts that are to be used as written—like **VAR**, and those parts that are replaced by one of a general set of things—like 'data type'. There is another problem in defining the **VAR** statement and that is that the **VAR** statement can be continued indefinitely. For example, you can write:

   VAR variable name1,variable name2, . . . variable namen:
        data type1;

If you were completely new to Pascal then you might find this definition very difficult to understand. Do you have to number the variable names one, two, three and so on? Do you write the row of dots before the data type? These questions may seem silly but they can be genuine causes of confusion when trying to understand the definition of a new Pascal statement.

Syntax diagrams

It is clear that it would be an advantage to have a more precise way of describing Pascal statements. A very easy to use and un-

146

ambiguous definition can be obtained by using syntax diagrams. The best way to gain an understanding of these is by a short example. The syntax diagram for the **VAR** statement is:

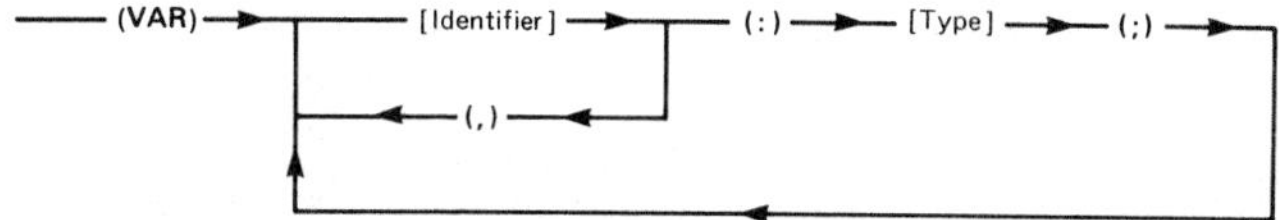

To make use of this diagram the first thing to notice is that anything between curved brackets () is quoted exactly as written in an example of the statement and anything between square brackets [] is replaced by an example of the sort named in the brackets. An example of the statement defined by the syntax diagram can be produced by treating the lines as a railway track and following a route through the diagram writing down everything between () as you meet it and writing down something of the correct sort for every [] you meet. (Notice that you must travel in the direction of the arrows—this is one-way track!)

Starting at the beginning the first thing to be encountered is (**VAR**) and then a branch that cannot be taken because it would mean travelling against the arrows. Moving on we meet a square bracket that has to be replaced with a valid identifier, 'total' say. Our statement so far is:

VAR total

After the identifier we can either travel on in a straight line or take a branch back to the beginning of the [identifier]. If we take the branch we meet (,) which means that we must write a comma and then we can write another valid identifier—'count' say. Our **VAR** statement now looks like:

VAR total,count

We can carry on going around this loop for as long as we like— each time round we are forced to write a comma and another variable name. If we have written enough variable names then we travel straight on and meet the (:) and then [type]. The : is written into the statement and type is replaced by an example of a data type— INTEGER, for example. Our statement now looks like:

VAR total,count:INTEGER

If you look at the rest of the diagram you should be able to see that after a semicolon you can loop back and define another list of variables as being another (or the same) data type without writing another **VAR**. Our statement could become:

    VAR total,count:INTEGER;
        area,cost:REAL;

Notice that you have to conclude the statement with a semicolon.

This short example of a syntax diagram should convince you that it solves all of the problems of defining the form of a general statement. By following a logical path through the diagram you can produce all the possible statements and see where repeats are possible, etc. Also, any statement that you write must correspond to a journey through the diagram—so you can check the correctness of anything you have written.

It is worth becoming familiar with syntax diagrams if only to be able to verify any statement that you have written. This chapter concludes with a complete list of syntax diagrams. It is important to notice that where there are any discrepancies, the diagrams in your manual (i.e. those specific to the version of Pascal that you are using) are probably correct.

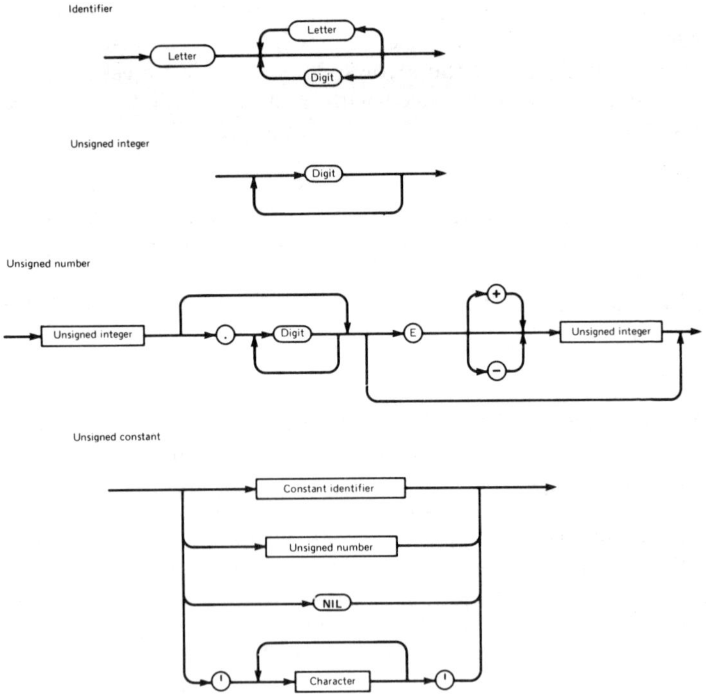

Constant

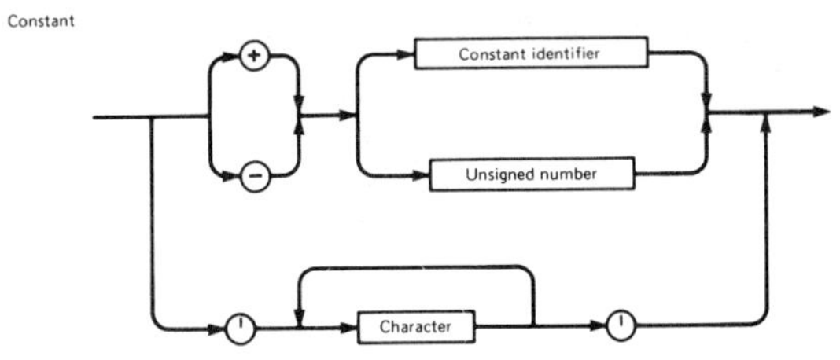

Simple type

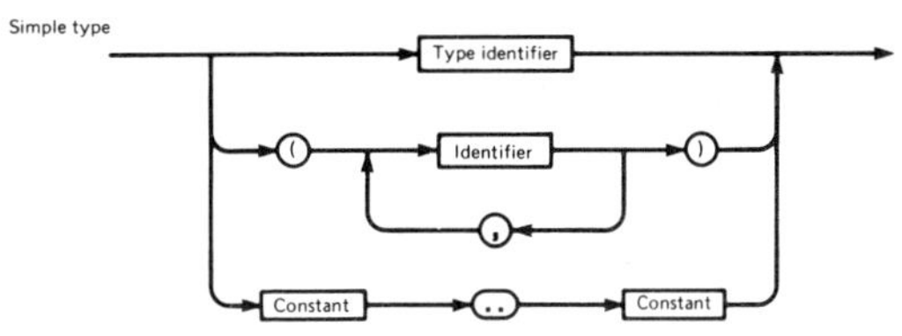

Type

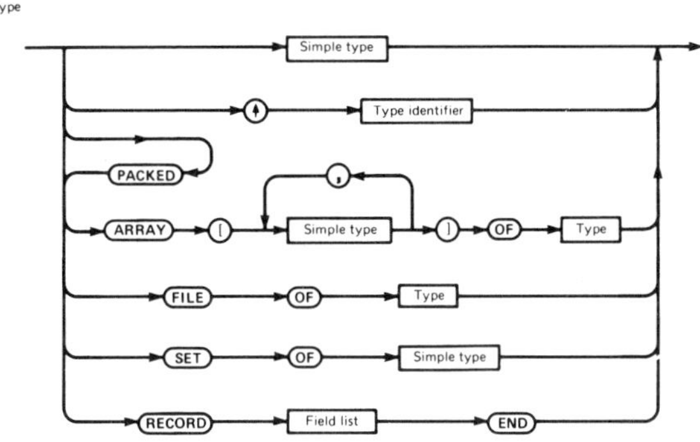

Field list

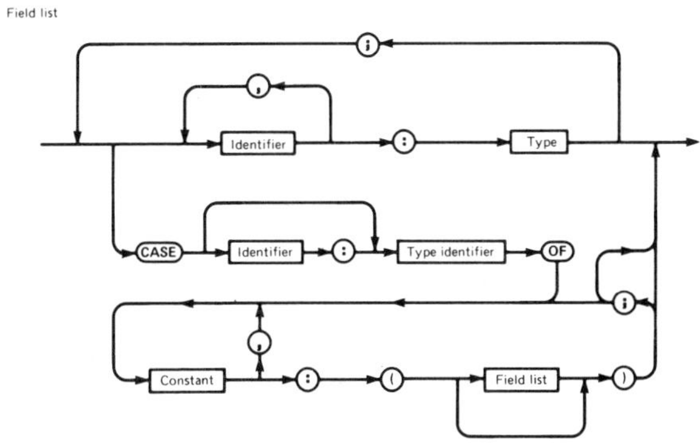

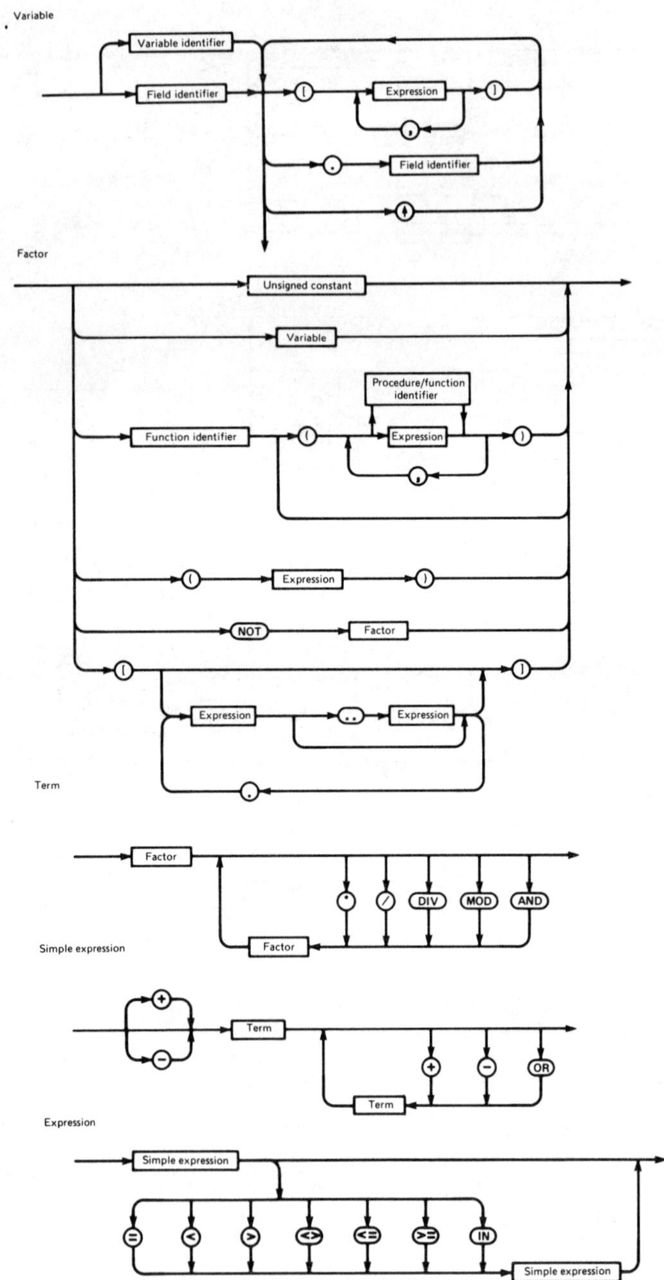

Variable
Variable identifier
Field identifier
Expression
Field identifier
Factor
Unsigned constant
Variable
Function identifier
Procedure/function identifier
Expression
Expression
NOT
Factor
Expression
Expression
Term
Factor
DIV
MOD
AND
Factor
Simple expression
Term
OR
Term
Expression
Simple expression
IN
Simple expression

Parameter list

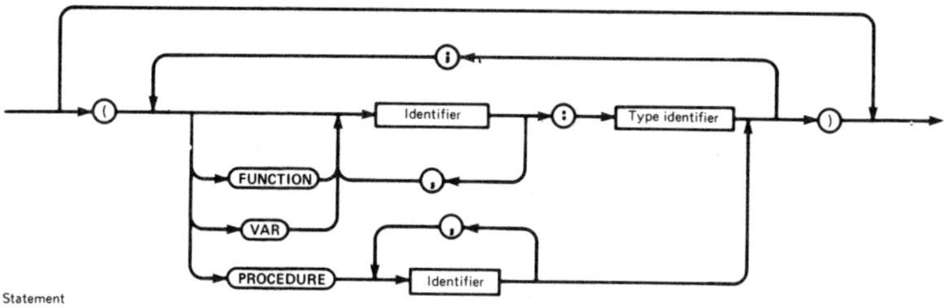

Statement

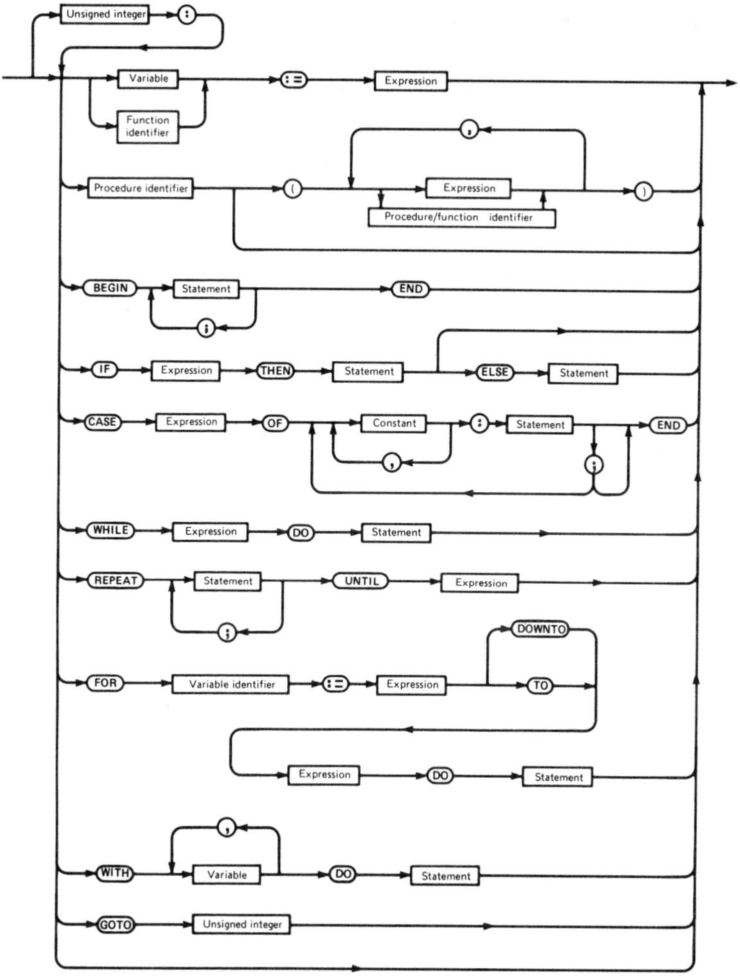

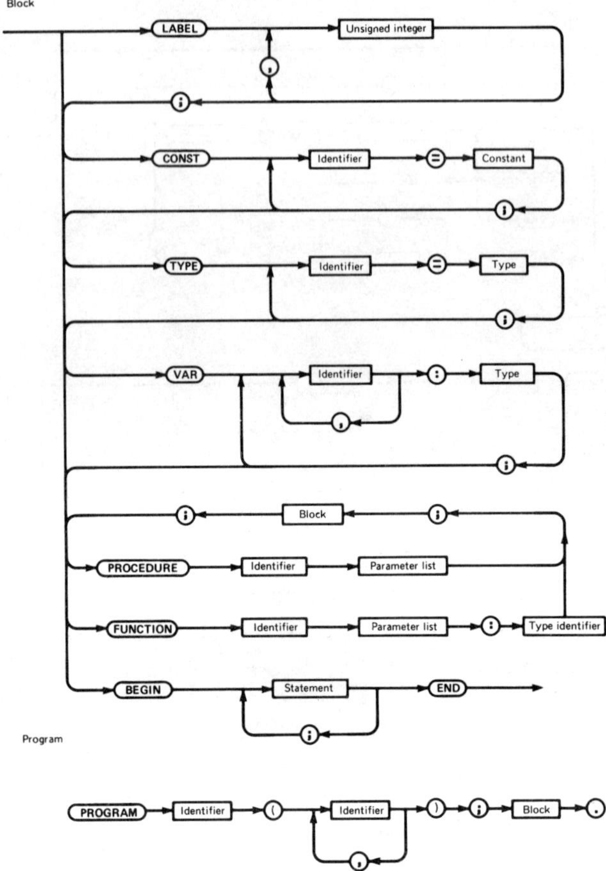

Summary

In this short chapter we have examined the problems of defining a
computer language. The syntax diagram was introduced as an easy
to understand and convenient solution. Syntax diagrams for all of
standard Pascal were presented.

Appendix 1

Pascal reserved words

AND	NIL
ARRAY	NOT
BEGIN	OF
CASE	OR
CONST	PACKED
DIV	PROCEDURE
DO	PROGRAM
DOWNTO	RECORD
ELSE	REPEAT
END	SET
FILE	THEN
FOR	TO
FUNCTION	TYPE
GOTO	UNTIL
IF	VAR
IN	WHILE
LABEL	WITH
MOD	

UCSD reserved words

INTERFACE
IMPLEMENTATION
SEGMENT
SEPARATE
UNIT

Appendix 2

Operator precedence

Operator	*Precedence*
NOT	Level 3 (highest)
*** / DIV MOD AND**	Level 2
+ − OR	Level 1
= < > <= >= <> IN	Level 0

Appendix 3

Predefined identifiers

	CONSTANT	TYPE	FUNCTION	PROCEDURE	FILE
ABS			×		
ARCTAN			×		
BOOLEAN		×			
CHAR			×		
CHR		×			
COS			×		
EOF			×		
EOLN			×		
EXP			×		
FALSE	×				
GET				×	
INPUT					×
INTEGER		×			
LN			×		
MAXINT	×				
NEW				×	
ODD			×		
ORD			×		
OUTPUT					×
PACK				×	
PAGE				×	
PRED			×		
PUT				×	
READ				×	
READLN				×	
REAL		×			
RESET				×	
REWRITE				×	
ROUND			×		
SIN			×		
SQR			×		
SQRT			×		
TEXT		×			
TRUE	×				
TRUNC			×		
UNPACK				×	
WRITE				×	
WRITELN				×	

Appendix 4
Some popular implementations of Pascal

UCSD Pascal

In UCSD Pascal each I/O device is called a volume and is given a volume name. For example, the screen is called

CONSOLE

the printer is called

PRINTER

and if the system has two disk drives they are usually called

DISK1 and DISK2.

Any file stored on a disk has to be given an external file name. An external file name is made up of three parts,

volume name.name.suffix

The 'volume name' is the name of the I/O device that the file is on, 'name' is the name of the file (up to 15 letters long) and 'suffix' indicates the type of the file. The most important types that UCSD recognises are:

.TEXT—text file
.BACK—back-up copy of a text file
.CODE—executable code
.DATA—data file

Examples of valid UCSD file names are:

DISK1. MYDATA. DATA
DISK2. CHAPTER1. TEXT

UCSD Pascal associates external file names with internal file names by using extended forms of RESET and REWRITE rather than through the program header:

RESET(internal name,'external filename')

156

and

REWRITE(internal name, 'external filename')

For example, if 'F' is the internal file name, then the following are valid:

RESET(F,'DISK1.MYDATA.DATA')
REWRITE(F,'DISK2.CHAPTER1.TEXT')

The action of RESET and REWRITE is the same as in standard Pascal but they now serve to make the link between internal and external file names.

The only additional procedure that we need to know about is CLOSE. In UCSD when you are finished with a file you must tell the system by using

CLOSE(internal filename,parameter)

The exact action of CLOSE depends on what 'parameter' is. Four values are possible but the three most useful are:

normal—if file is open for write then delete it
lock   —if file is open for write make it permanent
purge —remove the file from the disk

For example:

CLOSE(F,LOCK)—close F and make it permanent

To convert a standard Pascal program to UCSD requires only two changes:

1. Remove external file definitions from the program heading and add the external file name to any RESET or REWRITE in the program.
2. Add an appropriate CLOSE for each file used in the program.

UCSD Pascal also includes other extensions to standard Pascal, in particular it can handle random access files, but these are beyond the scope of this book.

Pascal M/MT+

Both these Pascals are similar to UCSD Pascal in that they use

RESET(internal file name,'external file name')

and

REWRITE(internal file name,'external file name')

to associate internal files with external files. They also use CLOSE to close a file. The only real difference is that the form of the 'external filename' varies according to the operating system being used. For example, in CP/M file names have three parts:

'disk':filename.extension

where disk is A,B,C, etc; filename is any name up to eight letters long; and extension is a three-letter name indicating the file type, for example:

.TXT for text
.BIN for binary
.DAT for data

A valid CP/M filename is:

A:Chap1.TXT

or

B:mydata.DAT

As in the case of UCSD Pascal, Pascal M and Pascal MT+ also have random access file facilities but a description of these is beyond the scope of this book.

Pascal Z

Pascal Z handles files in much the same way as UCSD Pascal. External file names are associated with internal file names using RESET and REWRITE, but there is no facility for CLOSEing files. All files are closed at the end of a Pascal/Z program:

—files that are open for read are left as they were
—files open for writing are made permanent

but there is no way to close a file explicitly.

External filenames are as in the case of Pascal M and MT+ dependent on the operating system used.

An important difference between Pascal Z and other Pascals is that it does not provide GET and PUT but only READ and WRITE.

TCL Pascal

TCL Pascal uses the extended versions of RESET and REWRITE

158

(see UCSD) to associate internal and external file names. The main difference between TCL and other Pascals is the form of the external file names. On the PET any device can be accessed using an external file name of the form

devicenumber,secondary address

or

devicenumber,secondary address,filename

For example:

REWRITE(printer,4,256)

associates the file 'printer' with the PET printer—device 4, secondary address 256.

Answers to questions

Chapter 2

1. Draw the line between the line starting **VAR** and the line starting **BEGIN**.

2. One. The statements between **BEGIN** and **END** form a single compound statement.

3. To make 'addthree' into 'addfive' change the line 'number:=3' into 'number:=5'.

4.

```
PROGRAM add(INPUT,OUTPUT);
VAR number1,number2,total:INTEGER;
BEGIN
        READ(number1);READ(number2);
        total:=number1+number 2;
        WRITE(total)
END.
```

Chapter 3

1. 20,2,2,2,0.5

2. The number of letters in a word cannot be fractional so it is best to use an INTEGER to store it:

   VAR nletters:INTEGER

however, the length of a piece of string can be fractional so it is best to use a REAL to store it:

   VAR len:REAL

For the same reasons temperature is best stored in a REAL and the number of people on a bus is best stored in an INTEGER. The definitions of all four variables can be combined into one **VAR** statement:

   VAR nletters,nbus:INTEGER;len,temp:REAL

160

3.

```
PROGRAM square(INPUT,OUTPUT);
VAR area,side:REAL;
BEGIN
        WRITELN;
        READ(side);
        area:=side*side;
        WRITELN;
        WRITE(area)
END.
```

Chapter 4

1.

```
PROGRAM sumprod(INPUT,OUTPUT);
CONST num=10;
VAR number,sum,prod:REAL;
                    i:INTEGER;
BEGIN
        sum:=0;
        prod:=1;
        WRITELN;
          FOR i:=1 TO num DO
                    BEGIN
                            READ(number);
                            sum:=sum+number;
                            prod:=prod*number
                    END;
        WRITELN;
        WRITE(sum);
        WRITELN;
        WRITE(prod)
END.
```

2. a<>b, 2*a<>6 and 2*a>=10 are true.

3.

```
IF taxcat=1 THEN rate:=0.3
                ELSE IF taxcat=2 THEN rate:=0.6
                                ELSE IF taxcat=3
                                        THEN rate:=0.9;
```

4.

```
i:=1;
WHILE i<=n DO BEGIN WRITE(i);i=i+1 END
```

Chapter 5

1. Change the line beginning with **CONST** to read:

CONST rate=0.2

2. After the line beginning READ(amount) insert

IF amount<0 **THEN**
                    BEGIN

and add an extra **END** before **END**.

3. The total amount saved in 'time' years is 12*time*amount, and subtracting this from the final sum in the bank gives the interest earned. Using this information the program can be changed to print the amount saved and the interest earned by adding

```
interest:=total−12*time*amount;
total:=12*time*amount;
WRITELN;
WRITE(total);
WRITELN;
WRITE(interest)
```

before the final **END**.

Chapter 6

1.

```
PROGRAM squroot(INPUT,OUTPUT);
VAR root:REAL;i,sq:INTEGER;
FOR i:=1 TO 20 DO
    BEGIN
            root:=SQRT(i);
            WRITELN;
            WRITE(root);
            sq:=SQR(i);
            WRITELN;
            WRITE(sq)
    END
END.
```

2. The largest of four numbers can be found by finding the larger of two pairs and then the larger of the resulting pair. To find the largest of a,b,c,d:

```
temp1:=max(a,b);
temp2:=max(c,d);
answer:=max(temp1,temp2)
```

As the parameter of a function can be an expression we can simplify the above and avoid the use of 'temp1' and 'temp2' :

```
answer:=max(max(a,b),max(c,d))
```


3. There are two ways of answering this question. You could use the idea introduced in question 2 to find the largest of four numbers to define a function that uses:

```
answer:=max(max(a,b),c)
```

A more straightforward solution is to completely rewrite the max function to accept three parameters:

```
FUNCTION max(a,b,c:REAL):REAL;
VAR temp:REAL;
BEGIN
        IF a>b THEN temp:=a ELSE temp:=b;
        IF c>temp THEN temp:=c;
        max:=temp
END
```


4.

```
PROCEDURE maxmin(a,b,c:REAL;VAR small,big:REAL);
VAR temp1,temp2:REAL;
BEGIN
        IF a>b THEN BEGIN temp1:=a;temp2:=b END
                ELSE BEGIN temp1:=b;temp2:=a END;
        IF c>temp1 THEN temp1:=c;
        IF c<temp2 THEN temp2:=c;
        big:=temp1;
        small:=temp2
END
```


5. Only 'a' and 'b' are changed in the main program because they are both global to procedure 'one'.

Chapter 7

1. True,false,true,true.
2.

```
VAR ans:CHAR;
    result:BOOLEAN;
    months:(jan,feb,mar,apr,may,jun,jul,aug,sep,oct,nov,dec);
    hour24:0..23;
    hour12:1..12;
```

3.

```
TYPE year=(jan,feb,mar,apr,may,jun,jul,aug,sep,oct,nov,dec);
     time24=0..23;
     time12=1..12;
```

4.

```
FOR ch:='a' TO 'z' DO WRITE(ch)
```

(assuming of course that 'ch' is of type CHAR.)

Chapter 8

1.

```
TYPE days=(mon,tue,wed,thu,fri,sat,sun);
VAR data1:FILE OF INTEGER;
    info:TEXT;
    year:FILE OF days;
```

2.

```
PROGRAM show(INPUT,OUTPUT,note);
VAR note:TEXT;
    ch:CHAR;
BEGIN
    RESET(note);
    WHILE NOT EOF(note) DO
        BEGIN
            READ(note,ch);
            IF NOT EOLN(note) THEN WRITE(ch)
            ELSE WRITELN
        END
END.
```

Chapter 9

1.

```
TYPE day=(mon,tue,wed,thur,fri,sat,sun);
     days=1..31;
VAR tempbath:ARRAY [1..6] OF REAL;
    tempday:ARRAY day OF REAL;
    name:ARRAY [1..20] OF CHAR;
    calendar:ARRAY month OF days
```

2.

```
TYPE date=RECORD
              day:1..31;
              mon:(jan,feb,mar,apr,may,jun,july,
                   aug,sept,oct,nov,dec);
              year:INTEGER
          END;
     digit='0'..'9';
     direc=(N,S,E,W);
VAR  birthrec:RECORD
                 name:ARRAY [1..20] OF CHAR;
                 birth:date
              END;
     bank:RECORD
             accno:ARRAY [1..6] OF digit
             amount:REAL
          END;
     weather:RECORD
                rain:REAL;
                winddir:direc;
                windspeed:REAL
             END;
```

3.

```
TYPE colour=(red,yellow,green);
VAR  light:SET OF colour;
```

STOP is '[red]' and GO is '[green]'. The empty set could be used to
represent a failed traffic light!

4.

```
FOR i:=1 TO 10 DO
    FOR j=1 TO 10 DO a[i,j]:=0
```

Chapter 10

1.

```
    PROCEDURE readday(x:day);
    VAR inp:PACKED ARRAY [1..3] OF CHAR;
        i:INTEGER;
        ch:CHAR;
    BEGIN
        FOR i:=1 TO 3 DO
                BEGIN
                        READ(ch);
                        inp[i]:=ch
                END;
        IF inp='mon' THEN x:=mon;
        IF inp='tue' THEN x:=tue;
        IF inp='wed' THEN x:=wed;
        IF inp='thr' THEN x:=thr;
        IF inp='fri' THEN x:=fri;
        IF inp='sat' THEN x:=sat;
        IF inp='sun' THEN x:=sun
    END;
```

2.

```
    PROCEDURE conexp(number:REAL;VAR frac:REAL;VAR
    exp:INTEGER);
    BEGIN
        exp:=0;
        WHILE number<1.0 DO
                BEGIN
                        number:=number*10.0;
                        exp:=exp-1
                END;
        frac:=number
    END;
```

3.

```
    PROCEDURE init(x:ARRAY [1..8,1..8] OF squares)
    VAR row,col:INTEGER;
    BEGIN
        FOR row:=1 TO 8 DO
                FOR col:=1 TO 8 DO
                        IF ODD(row) AND ODD(col)
```

                    THEN x[row,col]:=black
                    ELSE x[row,col]:=white;
    END;

4.

```
PROGRAM letcount(INPUT,OUTPUT);
TYPE upper='A'..'Z';
VAR letter:upper;
     num:INTEGER;
     used:ARRAY upper OF INTEGER;
BEGIN
     FOR letter:='A' TO 'Z' DO used[letter]:=0;
     (*Read in each letter of sentence and
                         add one to array element*)
     WRITELN;
     WHILE NOT EOLN DO
          BEGIN
                    READ(letter);
                    used[letter]:=used[letter]+1
          END;
     WRITELN;
     (*print out number of times each letter used*)
     FOR letter:='A' TO 'Z' DO
          BEGIN
                    num:=used[letter];
                    WRITELN('number of times   ';
                              letter;'   used =    ';num)
          END
END.
```

Chapter 11

1.

```
PROGRAM ques(INPUT,OUTPUT);
VAR ans:CHAR;
BEGIN
     REPEAT
        WRITE('what is your answer?');
        READ(ans)
     UNTIL (ans='Y' OR ans='N')
END.
```

2.

```pascal
TYPE marstat=(married,single);
VAR info=RECORD
              age:1..150;
              CASE status:marstat OF
                      married:(spousnam:PACKED ARRAY
                          [1..20] OF CHAR
                              time:0..100);
                      single:(nextkin:PACKED ARRAY
                          [1..20] OF CHAR)
          END
```

3.

```pascal
info.age:=40;
info.status:=married;
info.spousnam:='J SMITH              ';
info.time:=10

info.age:=20;
info.status:=single;
info.nextkin:='M BROWN              ';
```

Index